What Makes Us
Stronger

Stronger

What Makes Us
Stronger

FREYA LEWIS

SEVEN DIALS

First published in Great Britain in 2020 by Seven Dials
This paperback edition published in 2022 by Seven Dials
an imprint of The Orion Publishing Group Ltd
Carmelite House, 50 Victoria Embankment
London EC4Y 0DZ

An Hachette UK Company

1 3 5 7 9 10 8 6 4 2

A CIP catalogue record for this book is
available from the British Library.

ISBN (paperback) 978 1 8418 8348 9
ISBN (ebook) 978 1 8418 8349 6

Typeset by Born Group
Printed and bound in Great Britain by Clays Ltd, Elcograf S.p.A.

MIX
Paper from
responsible sources
FSC® C104740

www.orionbooks.co.uk

For my beautiful Nell,
who will stay in my heart forever

CONTENTS

PART TWO

PART THREE

Prologue

In April 2017, one month before the terrorist attack on Manchester Arena that claimed twenty-two lives and injured more than one hundred others, my family and I went to Universal Studios in Los Angeles and Las Vegas for two weeks. There's a picture of us all dressed in T-shirts and shorts huddled underneath the iconic glitzy diamond-shaped 'Welcome to Fabulous Las Vegas' sign located – rather bizarrely – slap-bang in the middle of the palm-tree-lined interstate just before you hit the main strip. There's my dad, Nick, looking typically goofy with his pale chicken legs sticking out of his chino shorts, wearing that startled expression on his face he seems to have in every photograph, and my mum, Alison, smiling nervously underneath her blonde bobbed hair whilst trying to make herself look tinier than she is by hiding behind me, as she hates having her picture taken. Next to Dad is my

older sister, Georgia, towering a foot above me with her long flowing sun-bleached hair on her shoulders, whose relaxed smile seems to reflect the inner confidence that I've always been so in awe of. And then there's me, standing up straight in that self-conscious way that teenagers raised on Instagram do, hands clasped in front of me as if I were meeting the Queen, beaming into the camera.

Despite the fact that we queued up for forty-five minutes in the sweltering midday heat to take that photo, I love it because it reminds me that, just before a smiley tourist standing next to us took it, we were all in typical Lewis family mode: Mum and Dad with their cameras dangling around their necks ready to capture every moment, memory and smile of our family holiday; Georgia and I laughing hysterically at the surreal sight of a bunch of cheerleaders in sparkly blue outfits precariously performing a human pyramid next to the red and yellow sign just moments earlier.

That photo belongs to the time before: a time when my body was neat and whole, a time before trauma and grief, hospitals and surgery. Now is the time after. Some things are worse; I can say proudly and confidently that others are better. But the dynamic I see in that photo is still the same as it is now. My family have been my constant, original links in a chain that has grown and grown with paramedics, police, nurses, doctors, dentists, physios, friends, strangers

and well-wishers – stronger and stronger, ever since 22 May 2017.

I remember how lucky I am to be here every day.

When I look at that photo, I know that I'm the luckiest of all.

PART ONE

CHAPTER ONE

News

A barrage of noise crashed through my consciousness; clanking, shouting, murmurs of conversations. My first thought was that I was in a hotel somewhere abroad. Then I realised that I couldn't move my body and a creeping fear slid over me. My eyes felt so heavy, like they'd been zipped shut, but I forced them open. Through my smudged vision, I could see half-shapes floating around in the dark room. Everything was blurry, making me feel dizzy and sick. Squinting, I could make out drips, tubes, wires. A monotonous, high-pitched *beep*, *beep*, *beep* rang in my ears. A slight light was shining on my dad's face to my right, and I felt an instant wave of relief because I knew that if my parents were there, then everything would be all right.

Only, as my eyes adjusted to my dimly lit surroundings, I could see that he had his head in his hands. His

skin was pale and drained, his eyes heavy with bags pulling them down underneath. I felt scared again.

He looked up.

'Hi,' he said, then carried on talking to a woman in a blue uniform who I hadn't noticed until then. She broke away from the conversation and walked towards me.

'Freya, we're going to give you more feed now,' she said. I didn't say 'Yes' or 'No' because I had no idea what was going on, my head was too groggy.

I realised that there was a tube up my nose, and suddenly became aware that I was finding it hard to breathe, as if something heavy had been placed on my chest. The rest of my body felt completely numb and I felt trapped.

Gripped with terror, I lay staring at the ceiling as Dad started talking to me. I ran my tongue around my gums, and my stomach lurched as the usually smooth surface felt raw and fleshy. I felt too scared to speak out of this alien mouth, but my head was filled with questions and I needed to know.

'What happened?'

Dad paused for a beat and then replied gently, 'There was an attack at the Arena.'

To begin with, his words didn't sink in at all. Part of me was still convinced that we were in another country, but also another part of me didn't want to believe what he was saying. We lived in a small safe village where nothing bad could ever happen to you.

It couldn't be possible. But, no matter how much I tried to ignore him, my mind wandered away from where we were – not a hotel, but a hospital – back to the concert, raking through my thoughts and trying to unpick the muddle of images, figures, noises. Slowly, I started to remember that I had been walking with someone, and as I lay there, I felt a strange sense of emptiness, like a part of me was missing. I started to remember a blush-pink top, and denim shorts, and then I remembered that I had been with my best friend, Nell.

Gradually, these fragments of memories started to slot together, like pieces of a strange jigsaw puzzle. We had been at the Ariana Grande concert together, and something terrible had happened: a bomb. I was hurt, was put in an ambulance, but Nell . . . I couldn't remember what had happened to Nell.

I assumed she must be here with me somewhere on this ward. 'Dad, where's Nell?' I croaked, finding it hard to get the words out, as if I had lost the ability to speak. I couldn't move my head much but I cast my eyes around the room as much as I could, expecting him to point towards the curtain sheltering the next bay.

He looked at me, then looked straight at the floor in silence. I had seen that expression once before, after my Granddad had passed away, and a twisted, acid knot of fear settled in the pit of my stomach. Tentatively, I repeated the question. 'Dad, where's Nell?'

He held my hand, and I saw his eyes were getting redder.

'Nell has died, Freya,' his voice was choked with tears.

I stared up at the ceiling, my brain flooded with confusion, absolutely convinced that she must be there with me. Dad started properly crying as I kept thinking, *This doesn't make sense. She can't be dead. She can't be dead.* I went into some sort of shock and in that moment, it felt like time stood still. I was aware that everything was still going on around me, but it was as if I couldn't hear or see anything as I tried to process the gravity of what Dad said, my brain struggling to believe it was true.

Then his words sunk into me so hard that it felt as if I'd been stabbed. A dull pain spread through my numbed body, all hope slowly draining from me.

This can't be happening . . . how can this be happening . . . ? We were just at the concert . . . we were singing . . . we were dancing . . . we were laughing . . . She told me . . . she told me . . .

It was too much to take in. Sinking into the sheets, I started to cry, patchy moments from the night terrorising my memories, as, in my groggy state, I tried to make sense of what was real, and what was not. I lay like this for two hours, lost in despair and confusion; my tears mingled with the most earth-shattering shock.

*

Later, Dad gently placed a small fluffy toy owl on my chest.

'Nell's mum dropped this off,' he said, his voice soft, trembling. 'It's Nell's, from when she was little. It was her favourite. Her mum wanted you to have it.'

I peered at the owl's cute beaky face, his fur matted in the way that only cuddly toys which have been hugged a thousand times over are, and vaguely remembered that I'd seen him on Nell's bed when we'd chatted on FaceTime.

I managed to reach over with my finger and stroke his little face. Dad gently put him next to my cheek, and I instantly smelled Nell and her home. It made me think about her family – particularly her mum – and I felt the first cold slaps of guilt which would haunt me for a long time to come: that I was here, when Nell wasn't.

How must she be coping?

A fresh wave of heartbreak climbed over me as the realisation began to dawn that I'd never see my beautiful friend's smiling face again. I scrunched my eyes shut tight, trying to block out the horrifying reality I had woken up to. There had been an explosion, and life would never be the same again.

CHAPTER TWO

Music

The first singer I ever saw live was Miley Cyrus at Manchester Arena. I was seven, my sister, Georgia, was ten, and we were hooked on *Hannah Montana*: a children's show where Miley plays a schoolgirl who transforms into a pop star at night.

We arrived at the Arena dressed in little Hannah Montana-inspired outfits – Georgia sporting a black trilby while I rocked a pink sparkly cap, with matching T-shirts – and clung closely to Mum and Dad as we navigated our way through the crowds of excited families and found our seats close to the stage. From my dinky vantage point, I peered upwards, marvelling at the dazzling set. It was like we had an entered a different world full of music, magic and make-believe. Miley kicked off the show in style by emerging out of a giant blue bubble and, halfway through her mesmerising performance, rode a motorbike swinging over our heads (not joking!) whilst belting out

the anthem 'I Love Rock 'n' Roll'. As I gazed up at the singer with my mouth gaping in an 'O' of wonder, a look of sheer, raw excitement painted on my face, I can still vividly remember my seven-year-old self thinking *This is the coolest thing ever!* Giddy and wide-eyed, Georgia was equally spellbound, and for most of the concert we stood in front of our seats, singing our little hearts out and dancing along.

Without doubt, it was one of our best moments as a family. After that, Mum and Dad would buy us concert tickets for presents every Christmas, and music became a big part of my life.

Over the years, our idols changed as often as our hairstyles, but the day One Direction appeared on *The X Factor* was a pivotal moment in my musical journey.

We live in a small, pretty village called Holmes Chapel, around half an hour's drive from Manchester. It's a friendly sort of place, with an olde-worlde high street lined with fairy lights, and home to a butcher's, florist and tea rooms. Rumours started flying around the village that someone from Holmes Chapel was going to be on the talent show, and I couldn't believe it when it turned out to be the shaggy-haired boy who'd gone to my high school and now worked in the local bakery on the high street: Harry Styles.

The X Factor had long since been a fixture of our Saturday nights. We would sit down on our squishy

brown leather sofas grouped around our TV in the front room, each with our favourite soft drinks to hand, and do what every family up and down the country would do: inch to the edge of our seats and keep our fingers crossed, beaming when the contestants were good and spitting out our drinks cringing when they were bad!

The night Harry Styles first performed with his band mates, the whole of Holmes Chapel was tuned in, and when I first saw him walk out on stage, I couldn't believe he was from our sleepy village. He looked like a proper pop star with a trendy (well, back then anyway!) grey cardigan and green silk scarf casually draped around his neck, a tumble of curls framing his face. And when he sang – well – I instantly fell in love.

'He's amazing!' I shrieked at the TV, eyes glued to the set.

From the night of 1D's first performance, I was their biggest fan, and my passion for music continued to grow as quickly as the fivesome rocketed up the charts.

A couple of years on, Ariana Grande nudged onto my playlist. School was buzzing about a new musical American teen sitcom, *Victorious*, about an aspiring singer, Tori Vega, and how she navigates life at a performing arts school. Ariana played her friend, Cat, and she was my favourite character because she reminded me of myself – a bit silly at times. Before long, Ariana started releasing her own music, and I thought her vocals were incredible. Georgia and I

would listen to her songs on repeat and when she announced her first tour, I begged Mum if it could be my Christmas present for that year. I firmly believe that it's only when you see someone perform live that you can truly see how good they are, and as Mum, Georgia and I bopped away to Ariana's infectious set, I was completely mesmerised by her performance. From then on, along with One Direction, Ariana became my top artist, and when she announced dates for her next tour, Dangerous Woman, performing at Manchester Arena on Monday 22 May 2017, my parents knew exactly what to surprise me with at Christmas: two tickets. I thought they were for Georgia and me, but there was one more surprise in store.

'You can take a friend with you this time, instead of going with us,' Mum said.

'What?!' I shrieked in disbelief. It felt like such a grown-up thing to do, go to a concert on my own for the first time with a friend. Now it was just a case of choosing who to go with.

CHAPTER THREE

Fall-out

Waking up to find your bed is moving is disconcerting, but not unusual when you're in hospital. Two days after finding myself in the Intensive Care Unit, I was transferred to a different ward. I made the most of looking up at the ceiling as it changed. Since waking up in hospital, the ceiling had become my happy place. I studied the cracks, the shapes they made – mostly triangles, I noticed – and counted the lines etched into the surface. I had no idea ceilings had so much character, like a craggy face with lots of stories to tell. I realised I'd never given my ceiling at home much thought, but then again, why would I have? Let's be honest, my time had more likely been spent watching make-up tutorials on YouTube and swapping Snapchats with my friends.

In May 2017, I was fourteen and in year nine at school. Studying for GCSEs began the following year,

so life at that point in time centred around my friends and family. My biggest passions were music, make-up, writing and drama – no surprise, really, having been brought up on an intoxicating mix of noughties pop music and *Coronation Street*. My dream has always been to become an actress, so every Saturday I'd slip into a different character at Actor Tribe, a performing arts class run by ex-*Corrie* stars Lee and Jenny.

Any life has its ups and downs, and I hadn't been a teenager for long; there were plenty of friendship squabbles that would die down as quickly as they blew up, and I had my fair share of insecurities. But life was good and I could feel myself inching towards adulthood, being given more independence and freedom by my parents bit by bit. Then, in the space of a few hours, I'd become like a baby again, unable to move or do anything for myself, a feeding tube snaking up my nose and down the back of my throat, a catheter bag dangling next to my bed.

As I was pushed along, I noticed the ceiling getting brighter and brighter and finally we stopped next to a window; though, from my fixed, horizontal position, I couldn't see out of it. Two trainee nurses were talking to Dad about where we lived, and when they confessed they'd never heard of Holmes Chapel, Dad, who's renowned for being a tad theatrical, boomed out in mock horror, 'What?! You've never heard of Holmes Chapel? Are you serious!'

Usually, I would have cringed at this – his trademark goofy antics – but as I lay there, I felt the tiniest twinge of happiness to hear him being his usual silly self beside me. It made me feel safer in the unfamiliar world I'd been plunged into, a world where nothing made sense, nothing felt the same, least of all my body.

I thought back to when we were in primary school, when it was actually considered to be really 'cool' to break a bone and end up in hospital. On the rare occasion that a classmate hobbled down the corridor with their leg in a cast or arm in a sling, they were instantly met with wide-eyed wonder and catapulted to celebrity status. And on a sunny spring day, when I was around eight, I got my first proper chance to be in the spotlight. Georgia and I were playing on the trampoline in our back garden. Springing into the air, I lost balance, fell awkwardly and crashed face-down on to the bouncy netting. I cried out in pain, and tears sprung into my eyes as my little nose, which had borne the brunt of the fall, turned Rudolf-red and started to throb.

'Mum, Dad, quick!' Georgia yelled as I clutched my hands over my face, wailing. My parents ran over, took one look at me and bundled us off to hospital. My injury looked worse than it was and the doctor reassured Mum and Dad that no serious damage had been done.

'Put some ice on it and she'll be fine,' he smiled.

But, of course, the next day at school, I couldn't resist embellishing my trampoline tumble.

'Guess what?' I said, to the pint-sized captivated audience gathered around me. 'I had to go to hospital yesterday . . . I broke my nose.'

By then, I was sporting a large purple shiner, and, as I was met by a chorus of 'ooohs' and 'ahhhs' from my classmates, I proudly strutted around the playground feeling quite the superstar.

I didn't feel like a celebrity this time. I was covered top to toe in one of those mint-green hospital blankets I'd seen on *Casualty*, but underneath was a different story. At some point in the ICU, drifting in and out of consciousness, I remember glancing down at myself and seeing that I was covered in plaster. There were individual plaster casts on each of my fingers, a cast all the way down my right arm, and on my left leg. My neck was fixed upright (probably another reason why I'd become so well acquainted with the ceiling) so I couldn't turn my head.

But out of the corner of my eye, I'd managed to catch a glimpse of my left arm, which had given me the biggest shock of all.

A row of large metal rods jutted out of the entire length of my limb. When I first saw it, I thought I was hallucinating and had turned into some sort of weird mummy-cum-robot, but before I could think about it any further, I'd fallen back to sleep.

Now, as I settled into my new home – the High Dependency Unit – I was starting to become a bit more

aware of my surroundings. It was quieter here – not *quiet* by any stretch, but less crashing, banging and shouting – and the comforting sound of my parents' chatter made me feel a lot calmer. I was still incredibly drowsy and numb from all the medication I was on, a jumble of painkillers and antibiotics. But I was starting to understand the full extent of what had happened to me that night, though the attack and the loss of Nell were too painful to think about just yet, and I kept them locked away in an airtight box deep in the back of my mind.

At one point I remember Mum sitting next to me and telling me about my arm.

'It's been very badly injured,' she said, her voice soft. 'Part of your bone is missing, so that's why you have a frame on it. It will stay there to keep your arm fixed in place while the bone grows back.'

In my foggy brain, I thought, *If there is a bit of bone missing, then where's my arm?*

But it was through chats like this, married with snatches of conversations I overheard from the fleet of specialists who came to see me, and memories that drifted back from the night itself, that I came to know of the damage inflicted on my body and what had happened to me during those first few days after I arrived at hospital.

In total, I had twenty-nine separate injuries from head to toe. These included a shattered left arm with an open fracture of my humerus (the long bone at the top of

the arm), two broken legs (a fractured right ankle and a broken left tibia, aka shinbone), a shrapnel wound to my left eye, a perforated eardrum, broken nose, busted mouth, loss of several teeth, whiplash, contusion – aka bruising – to my left lung, nerve damage in my left hand, as well as multiple lacerations and burns all over my body.

Basically, there wasn't a part of my body which hadn't been affected by flying shrapnel from the bomb.

When I was first rushed to Royal Manchester Children's Hospital on the night of the attack, I was immediately taken for X-rays and tests. I remember opening my eyes and seeing these boxes coming over my head and voices saying 'We're just going to do a scan now.' As I was moved into different positions, agonising pains shot through my body. I remember getting increasingly frustrated with everyone; I think I was on so many painkillers and in so much shock that I couldn't understand why they wouldn't stop and let me go to sleep.

When I came out of the X-ray department, disorientated, afterwards, I have a distinct memory of turning my head as much as I could to see my Mum sitting there, holding my hand. She was crying, her face red and puffy. I could see the distress and panic weighing her down and I felt distraught, as I'd never seen her like that before. It was in that moment that it really hit me how much was wrong.

A surgeon came in soon after and said, 'We're taking her to theatre now, we've found traces of metal in her stomach area.' Mum held my hand tightly.

I looked up and, blinking through sore eyes, saw that they were all wearing what looked like shower caps on their heads.

I called out wildly, 'I don't want a scar across my stomach, Mum!'

'Don't worry,' Mum stroked my hand with the lightest of touches, understanding what I couldn't; that scars weren't important now. 'I love you.'

Her face grew distant as the room got smaller and everything went black.

I learned later that doctors spent ten and a half hours intricately bolting, drilling, sewing and bandaging me back together that morning. They had no idea what state I'd be in when I woke up from surgery, whether I would be left brain-damaged or able to walk again.

This was the first time the staff at the Royal Manchester Children's Hospital had to deal with the devastating effects of a bomb blast and military doctors had been called in to help. As it turns out, it wasn't fragments of shrapnel they ended up removing from my stomach, but my own teeth and bone, which I'd swallowed during the impact of the attack.

After that first bout of major surgery, I was placed in an induced coma, and over the next few days, underwent two further operations. I can't begin to

imagine how my parents must have felt as I lay there with a ventilator machine breathing for me, a feeding tube running up my nose and being wheeled from one surgery to the next.

The last time they'd seen me, Nell and I were all dressed up, giggling and singing, barely able to contain our excitement as we went off arm in arm to our first concert together, taking our first steps towards adulthood.

CHAPTER FOUR

Nell

It was day two of secondary school. I was a nervous eleven-year-old, still finding my feet as a member of Year Seven, when this girl came bobbing up to me, all smiles and shiny brown hair.

'Hi, I'm Nell!' she said.

'Hi, I'm Freya,' I replied, shyly.

She had an aura about her, so happy and kind, and I was drawn to her. Later that day, we found ourselves in the same drama class, where we instantly bonded over our love of acting, make-up, fashion – and our mutual hatred of PE. She was, for me, one of those rare people you meet and instantly feel like you've known for years.

We were good friends from then on. Nell, full of warmth and affection, would always give me a hug when she saw me in the mornings or grab hold of my hand as we lined up for lessons. She was very funny,

and would pass me little jokes across the classroom table, while I tried to muffle my laughter with my hands before the teacher noticed. They didn't mind though. They knew we worked well together, and would often sit us together for projects. Nell was super smart, and didn't think twice about helping me out if I was struggling in class, correcting my spellings in assignments, inspiring me to try harder, do better. All of this earned her the nickname 'Mum', especially as she looked a lot older than me. If you were to put the two of us side by side – me: slight and petite with blonde hair framing a childish face, and Nell: a good few inches taller with fashionable dark-rimmed glasses and shiny dark brown hair – you'd never have guessed we were the same age.

Despite our Tom and Jerry looks, we were like two peas in a pod and would spend hours – and I mean hours – chatting on FaceTime after school about how to create the perfect winged eye liner, whether we liked the boy in our year's new haircut or not (Nell always used the term 'grim' to describe something she disliked) and everything in between. She very rarely got cross, but one thing that did drive her mad was when I didn't reply to her texts in thirty seconds. She'd text again saying: 'Freyaaaaa!!' and then, if I still didn't respond, 'FREYYAAAAA!!!!!' in shouty caps. She didn't care if people were mean to her – it was like water off a duck's back – but she'd go wild if someone was

nasty to me or any of her other friends, like a lioness protecting her cubs.

When my parents gave me the Dangerous Woman tickets and said I could take a friend, I knew straight away that she'd be my 'plus one'. She was an even bigger Ariana Grande fan than I was, and with her birthday just a month before the gig, it made the ideal present. Keeping it a secret from her for nearly five months was a struggle, however, especially as I knew how disappointed she was that she hadn't managed to get her hands on any tickets.

'I'm so gutted about Ariana,' Nell would sigh now and again.

'I know, it's such a shame,' I'd reply, using my best acting skills to look equally as disappointed whilst secretly smiling inside.

As the weeks rolled by, I was bursting to tell her, but at the same time, the build-up was making the surprise all the more exciting, like those anticipation-filled weeks edging closer to Christmas morning. Of course, being the mischievous friends that we were, I couldn't resist teasing her a little.

We'd be in drama class, and I'd whisper to her, 'I've got you the best present ever and you'll never guess what it is,' and she'd grip my arm playfully as if she was trying to squeeze it out of me.

Nell's birthday was on Easter Sunday, so I planned the surprise for when we got back to school the Monday

after. The night before, with 'Dangerous Woman' playing in the background, I copied and pasted pictures of Ariana Grande from the internet and printed them out on Dad's printer, then cut each one out and glued them to the envelope to make it look pretty. Mum came in and asked me what I was doing.

'I'm sorting Nell's present,' I told her proudly, showing off my handiwork.

I planned to give it to Nell when we met in the morning before our first lesson. We'd have an audience, as one of our other friends, Ellie, was in on the surprise and couldn't wait to see Nell's reaction when she opened her gift.

Ellie texted me in the morning, saying she was running late, putting the grand unveiling on hold as Nell and I hurried into Spanish together. We were sitting on different tables, but Nell was in my eye line, and knowing all would be revealed soon, was jostling in her seat with excitement.

'What is it?' she mouthed to me across the classroom.

'I'm not telling you!' I mouthed back, giggling.

As soon as the bell went, we ran out of the classroom with Ellie now in tow.

'Right, give it to me!' Nell squealed impatiently.

Grinning from ear to ear, I finally handed her the envelope.

She stared wide-eyed at the pictures on the front and then ripped it open. 'Oh my God!'

She screamed so loudly the Spanish teacher came rushing out of the classroom.

'Girls, what's going on?!' she asked, bewildered.

'Freya's got us Ariana Grande tickets!' Nell screamed, her voice reaching a new octave in her excitement, enveloping me in a huge bear hug and nearly toppling me off my feet.

'Thank you, thank you, thank you,' she said, her teary voice muffled as she buried her head in my shoulder.

For the rest of the day I basked in a halo of happiness as Nell jumped up and down telling everyone at school that we were going to see Ariana.

It was the first concert she'd ever get to go to, which made it all the more special.

CHAPTER FIVE
Kindness

When the doctors said they were going to remove my breathing tube and bring me out of the induced coma I'd been in for three days, my parents had to gather themselves for whatever state I'd be in when I woke up. They'd spent the days before sitting by my bedside, watching over me while not daring to sleep themselves. Now the question weighing heavily on their minds was: 'Will she still be the same Freya?'

The first time I came around, I was confused and disorientated. The noises of the hospital mingled with my memories of the arena and instead of realising that I was remembering the attack, I thought I was having some sort of terrible premonition. I cried out hysterically, warning my parents that we couldn't go to the concert as something horrible was going to happen. This was understandably very difficult for my parents to witness, but seeing me actually awake and talking – a

glimpse of the daughter they knew and loved – brought much-needed relief.

The second time I came to was a day later.

'Where am I going to eat?' I heard an annoyed voice say. Through my strange, fish-eye vision, I could make out Georgia talking to my dad. 'Can we go to McDonalds?'

Dad looked exasperated, 'We can't go to McDonald's again.'

Mum drifted into view, 'Yes, Georgia, we can't go to McDonald's again.'

Little did they know, they'd soon be bombarded with more home-cooked meals than they could ever eat as news of the atrocity rippled through the community and an army of people started dropping off trays of lasagne, cottage pies and vegetable bakes to feed the families of the victims and the medical staff who were working around the clock to care for them.

Waking up to this felt kind of normal; it just seemed like a typical Lewis family argument and because everything was so fuzzy, I thought I was having a dream. They noticed I was awake and, as their faces dipped in and out of focus, I could make out my parents gathering around me and stroking my head.

Dad's phone started ringing. He assumed it was the press, who'd been hounding them since a story about me had appeared in the papers, with news teams stationed outside the door of Royal Manchester

Children's Hospital and reporters waiting outside our house (Georgia was even chased up the road). So he brusquely questioned the caller – 'Harry who?!'

Then I could see a shadow of a phone being pushed toward me. 'It's Harry,' Dad hissed excitedly.

What? I thought, confused, then a familiar voice floated out of the speaker phone – 'Hello' – and it registered in my mind that it was Harry Styles. I was on the phone with Harry Styles. Overwhelmed, I started crying and crying.

'I love you,' I said, or I think I said, as the words didn't seem to come out right.

'I love you too,' he replied.

Then the dream slowly faded away and I drifted back into the warm embrace of sleep.

That surprise call was all down to my sister. She'd become the self-appointed Lewis family PA, running around behind the scenes answering questions from concerned family, friends, neighbours, teachers and keeping everyone updated on my progress. How she found the strength to do this while revising for her A levels and coping with the repercussions of the attack which had shaken our tiny village and devastated the lives of so many, I still don't know. Perhaps doing something practical *was* her way of coping.

Knowing how much I loved Harry Styles, she'd posted on her Facebook page saying that if anyone knew him, could they please pass on my dad's number

as it would be such a lift for me to talk to him. Living in such a close-knit community, the message had eventually reached Harry via the school and before we knew it, here he was on the line.

When I spoke to him on speakerphone, the sedatives were still surging around my system. A garbled 'I love you' is all I'd managed before I fell back to sleep again. But it meant so much to my family and everyone at the hospital, having a huge star like Harry get in touch out of the blue to offer his support.

Of course Dad, being the big softie that he is, started to cry. 'I can't believe it,' he sobbed, which set off one of my nurses, Beth, who had diligently cared for me in the ICU when I had arrived on the ward. While I was undergoing that first lot of major surgery, she was on hand comforting my parents, constantly checking in on them in the family room where they were huddled together, with other shaken families of children injured in the attack, making everyone endless cups of tea.

Then, after she heard that I was out of the operating theatre, she made sure I looked comfortable before my parents came to see me, straightening out my sheets, untangling all my tubes and wires, and lowering the bed so that Mum and Dad could sit with me and hold my hand. It sounds strange, fixing me up as I slept, but I learned that little things like that made all the difference to the families who have children in an ICU, bringing a semblance of calm and normality to a situation that

is anything but. After that, Beth became a comforting familiar fixture to Mum and Dad as she looked after me, carrying out my personal care, safety precautions and hourly checks.

All the while, droves of specialists were coming in to assess my injuries. After the first operation, the Army surgeons had told my parents that the key to the successful healing of blast wounds was to clean and re-dress them on a number of occasions to ensure that absolutely all the shrapnel had been removed before they were stitched. It really brought into focus just how potentially serious my wounds were and also that it would be a long process, involving a lot more surgery, before I could be considered to be on the road to recovery. It was a scary time for my parents and Beth, with her big smile and gentle nature, was always on hand for support.

As time went on, I also had the chance to see how many heroes there are in the world; a lot of them were at my school. Piles of brightly coloured envelopes were gathering on the doormat of our home in Holmes Chapel, and every time Georgia came to visit she'd arrive clutching a fresh bundle of Get Well Soon cards. As I couldn't move my arms – my right was trussed up in a splint, the left in the cumbersome frame – Georgia would read them out to me. She'd position herself in the high-backed chair next to my bed, carefully tear open the envelopes and show me each card before

reading out the heartfelt messages, trying to keep her voice steady.

'OK, so this one is from your maths class,' she said a couple of days into the High Dependency Unit, before reading out dozens of messages. 'Get better soon, Freya, we miss you so much, school isn't the same without you,' said one. My eyes filled with tears.

'Can't believe what has happened. Thinking of you, we love you,' said another. And so they continued, zigzagging across the page, each word of support, no matter how small, filling my heart. Soon rows of cards lined my room, and cuddly toys filled my bed, as if they were building a force field of strength around me, with Nell's fluffy owl nestled close to my head. As time passed, I became more and more desperate for those messages. They were my window into my old life; reminding me that I went to school and drama classes and flute lessons. The simple sound of the crinkling of the paper as Georgia slid her finger under the edge of the seal of the envelope, releasing the kindness encased within, became a soothing antidote to the constant high-pitched beeping of the monitors, the doctors coming in four times a day to do their various checks, the physios trying to make me do the simplest yet most impossible movements, the constant discussions about how best to dress my wounds and mend my broken bones, the nurses giving me a full bed bath each day, moving me every four hours so that I didn't get pressure sores on

my body, and a daily ritual of cleaning the pin sites of my external fixator – which was the most painful thing of all. They'd soak a wipe in disinfectant, and then rub the edges of my frame so it wouldn't fuse with my skin and cause infection. Worse still, they had to rip off the scabs that formed around each pin, making me scream out every time. As you can imagine, the cards became a welcome distraction.

All of these gestures and the people behind them became my lifelines, together forming crutches I could lean all my weight on. They were an incredible support for my parents as well. I thought a lot at the time, and I still do now, that because I was unconscious for the first few days, my parents were the ones who'd really suffered. I'll never forget the look on Dad's face when he had to tell me about what had happened to Nell – the pain it cost him. The look on Mum's face when I woke up briefly before that first surgery, so full of fear and panic. And their lives were on hold now – for me.

I knew I had to keep it together for my family. I absolutely hated seeing my parents in pain – it was the worst feeling. So the first night in the HDU, I made a silent vow that no matter how upset I was feeling or how scared I was, I had to put on a brave face for them. The truth was, I cared more for my family then I did for myself. I had to get better for them.

CHAPTER SIX

Scraps of Normality

In those early days, time seemed to crawl along at a snail's pace. Everything felt like it was happening in slow motion, as if I were floating along in a trance. The hours drifted by in a blur of sleep, check-ups and surgeries (or sometimes pretend-sleep if I didn't have the strength to talk to the doctors – but shhh, don't tell anyone).

I was cocooned in my own bubble, the only constant being the soothing presence of my family by my bedside. Mum and Dad were with me constantly, while Georgia came in every day after school.

Within a couple of days of being in the HDU, the individual dressings on my burned fingers were removed, and I discovered that one of my favourite things to do was hold Georgia's hands and stroke her manicured nails while she chatted to me.

Despite me being the more make-up-obsessed and self-conscious one out of the two of us, I had a terrible

habit of biting my nails, reducing them to a row of short stubs. But Georgia looked after hers beautifully, painting them in different colours. Holding her hands, feeling the sensation of the smooth varnish, a reminder of regular life outside the ward brought me much-needed solace.

One afternoon, she came in, plopped down next to me, and waggled her fingers at me.

'Look, Freya, I've got them purple today,' she said, smiling at me proudly. I couldn't move my neck, so I peered at her hand from the corner of my eye, and through my hazy vision carefully examined each of her nails, stretching over to brush my finger over the glossy surface. It was bliss.

Suddenly, I stopped on the fourth finger, felt a rough groove and wrinkled my brow.

'That one is chipped!' I blurted out in *faux* shock.

'Oh sorry, sorry!' Georgia gasped, quickly swiping her hand away to examine the damage for herself as I smiled at her cheekily. Seeing my face, she snapped, 'Freya – not funny!' but then she started to laugh.

It felt good to tease my sister in the way that I'd always done – despite what had happened, the old Freya was still in there somewhere.

I woke the next morning feeling a sense of relief. I'd been in hospital for nearly a week and a half, and it was one of the first days that I didn't have surgery. No

being prepped for the operating theatre with doctors running through the list of possible complications – paralysis, excessive bleeding, blood clots, heart attack; no waking up in a horribly disorientated state as I came around from the body-jangling anaesthetic.

As I blinked the sleep from my eyes, one of the nurses came in to check my vitals.

'Shall I put the TV on for you?' she asked, scribbling on her pad. 'Yes please,' I replied sleepily. She switched the monitor on above my bed and BBC news flashed up.

Ariana Grande's doll-like face filled the screen as I caught the tail-end of a news story about a charity concert she was organising in Manchester for the victims of the attack. The event was happening this coming Sunday. My breath quickened. I'd later come to see that it was a good thing, an act of solidarity, strength – and incredible kindness to fundraise for the innocent victims and their families – but in those raw, fragile days in the wake of the attack, I couldn't think of anything worse. The thought of another concert being held in Manchester made me feel physically sick.

Mum and Dad walked in just as I burst into tears. They glanced up at the TV, the colour draining from their faces, and quickly scrambled for the remote control to switch it off.

Mum rushed over and wrapped me in a hug.

'What's going on?' I sobbed into her shoulder.

'Don't worry, everything will be OK,' she whispered back, barely managing to get her words out through her own tears.

By the time Georgia came to see me later in the afternoon, my cheeks were sore from hot tears, my mood dark.

Mum filled her in on what happened, whilst throwing nervous glances in my direction, and she sat down next to me, taking a deep breath.

'I've been invited to the concert,' she said tentatively. 'But, I won't go if you don't want me to.'

I looked at her fearfully.

'No, Georgia, you can't,' I replied.

'OK, Baba, don't worry, I won't.'

As she said it, she squeezed my hand and gave me a reassuring smile. *Baba.* Hearing my old nickname made my nerves settle. Georgia used to call me 'Baba' when I was little, but we'd fallen out of the habit a few years ago, probably when I started turning into an annoying teenager and thought that I'd outgrown cutesy baby names. Now, though, it felt soothing and I managed a small smile.

My emotions were changing minute by minute.

That afternoon I received my first visitors: Auntie Elaine and my cousin, Kristian. Eight years older, he was like a big brother to me, and I felt a surge of happiness to see two familiar faces.

'KrisseeWissee!' I said excitedly as he walked in, adjusting his round dark-rimmed Harry Potter-esque glasses on his nose and giving my hand the tiniest of squeezes to avoid brushing against my burns.

'Hiya,' he smiled.

I found myself instinctively searching his face for a reaction – some sort of clue – to gauge how much I'd changed. Since arriving in hospital, I hadn't looked at myself in the mirror, I hadn't wanted to. Now, surrounded by my first visitors, I felt incredibly self-conscious about the state I was in.

Though the medication had numbed the pain from my injuries, my mouth didn't feel right at all, and I struggled to pronounce my 's's and 't's, making me sound like a drowsy five-year-old. I forced myself to power through. After all, talking was such a simple thing to do, and something I loved to do – usually, people couldn't shut me up – so I had to keep trying, even though it felt alien to me, to force the words out.

So, when Kristian asked me how it was going, I took a deep breath, and started chatting about something completely normal for the Lewis family . . . Dad's snoring.

'It's worse than having a broken arm,' I said, ignoring the weird sensation in my mouth, my tongue swimming around the gaps where my teeth should have been. 'When Dad's on the night shift, he sleeps next to me and keeps me awake all night!'

'Dad's snoring is really bad,' Georgia chipped in.

'Try sleeping next to him for thirty years,' Mum sighed, shaking her head.

'Oi! Stop ganging up on me!'

Dad stuck his bottom lip out in an exaggerated sad face but really I could tell he was enjoying the banter – we all were. The sound of our laughter floated down the hospital corridors and seeing so many smiles made me feel good; I'd succeeded in making everyone feel better. I took a mental picture of those smiles and stashed them away in my mind to pull out for later on in the night, when all was still and dark, and I was left alone with my turbulent thoughts.

'Glad to see you haven't lost your sense of humour!' Auntie Elaine wiped tears from her eyes. 'Oh, and before I forget, here, we brought you some presents.'

Digging into a gift bag, she pulled out a grey knitted Boofle bear and started looking around for a suitable home for it.

'It's like a zoo in here!' she exclaimed, pointing to the menagerie of soft animals around me – zebras, cats, elephants, dogs – stacked up in five big bags like Santa's sacks.

'I know! And they just keep coming,' Mum replied.

Auntie Elaine placed the bear in pride of place on a side table, and then pulled out a Disney Princess bottle with a straw. I couldn't help smiling. It looked like something you'd give a toddler.

'Your mum said it's tricky for you to drink at the moment, so I thought this might come in handy,' she said, displaying the cup in her hands as if she were on a game show.

'Thanks, Auntie Elaine. I love it,' I smiled, suddenly aware of how dry my mouth felt.

It actually felt dry all the time, like I hadn't drunk water in years. And, because of all my injuries, especially the whiplash, drinking out of a normal cup was impossible.

'Right, Freya, I think it's time for you to get some rest now.' Mum looked at me, brow furrowed, her face suddenly full of concern. You could tell by the intuitive way she cared for me that she used to be a nurse, but I couldn't imagine how difficult it must be to look after me under these circumstances. So I paid attention to everything she said, wanting to make her life as easy as possible.

'OK, Mum,' I replied obediently, smiling up at Kristian and Auntie Elaine. 'Thanks so much for coming to see me.'

'Don't be silly,' said Auntie Elaine, tucking her blonde hair nervously behind her ear as if she were remembering something. 'It's just so lovely to see you awake and smiling. You're so brave.'

Brave. The word bounced around in my head. I'd heard it a lot recently. But, I didn't feel brave. Surely I was just doing what anyone else would do in my situation?

I was later told that Auntie Elaine had come to see me in hospital the night of the attack. When she arrived, I'd just come out of the initial lot of surgery and was asleep in the ICU. One of the doctors had come in to examine my eyes and said, 'There's something in here. It needs to be taken out.'

Auntie Elaine had felt sick and Mum had to take her out. A couple of days later, she had brought my grandparents to see me but, worried she'd become upset again, had hung back in the side room while my grandma and granddad came on to my ward. When they saw me, they were apparently lost for words, but managed to sit with me for a while. My parents were surprised that they had managed to hold it together.

Back then, no one knew what condition I was going to be in post-op, so for Auntie Elaine to find me awake and talking the second time she mustered the courage to see me must have been such a relief.

'Look after yourself,' Kristian said. 'And don't let your dad's snoring keep you awake!'

He gave me a smile as he and Auntie Elaine headed off, waving at me until they disappeared through the ward doors.

CHAPTER SEVEN
Two Steps Forward

Georgia was the 'early night-shift leader' that evening. It meant she'd watch over me from 9 p.m. until around 2 a.m. when my parents came back, giving them a chance to get some rest over at the nearby Ronald McDonald House. But sleeping wasn't proving particularly easy for me.

That night, I had another one of my terrifying hallucinations. Since I'd arrived in the HDU, I was getting lost in this vivid world, somewhere between sleep and consciousness, where I imagined I was training to be a Dementor, the dark, evil creatures from *Harry Potter*, who suck out human happiness. Worse, Lord Voldemort was sitting next to me, sweeping a cloak across my shoulders and urging me to fly.

'I don't want to fly,' I mumbled out into the darkness, as Dad lay on the camp bed next to me (quietly snoring).

We'd been to Universal Studios in LA around three weeks before the attack, and had sat on the most terrifying ride in Harry Potter World where a whole load of these horrible Dementors came flying at you. I'd come out shaking. I think the fear I felt then must have become entangled in my mind with the darkness of the attack, resulting in these horrifying visions. I came back to reality in the early hours, my head pounding, nose stuffy, throat scratchy.

By the morning, my cold was joined by a migraine. My temples felt squeezed, stomach queasy. And as doctors had increased my feed to try and bolster me up, my tummy was doubly wobbly.

'I don't feel good,' I whimpered to Mum and Dad who were sat helplessly by my bedside. 'Everything hurts.'

'I know, babe,' Mum soothed, stroking my forehead. 'Close your eyes, it'll make you feel better.'

No sooner had the words escaped her lips than my lead surgeon, Matt, came in clutching a file. With his crisp white shirt and professional manner, he had a comforting air of authority about him, but he'd started greeting my parents as friends, revealing his soft side. He looked over at me, face full of concern.

'How is she doing? Is she back to her old self?'

My parent's nodded, water gathering in their eyes.

Matt's shoulders slumped, as if the weight of the world had been lifted from his shoulders, his worried expression crumpling into a look of relief. After

operating on me for so long on the night of the attack, he'd had grave concerns about the effects the injuries would have on my mind and body. Seeing how deeply he cared reassured my parents that I really was in the best possible place. And as we came to realise again and again in the months that followed, he wasn't the only one to care during those darkest hours. If the night of the 22nd had represented the worst of humanity, my parents were also starting to see the best.

Matt straightened up, an apologetic look in his eyes.

'I have the results of the X-rays we took yesterday,' he said. There's a small problem with the bone in Freya's right ankle,' he told us. 'It needs to go in a cast.'

My parents looked at one another, exchanging a silent 'here we go again' glance between them.

Before long, I had both legs in plaster. Now, with all four limbs bandaged up, my transformation into a mummy was *really* complete. I felt like I'd taken a couple of steps backwards, and even though I'd vowed to keep a brave face, I struggled to keep my spirits up.

Vicky, a physio, and Sarah, an occupational therapist, came by to do exercises with me every day once I'd been transferred to the HDU, trying to get me moving. They were both smiley and in their thirties; Sarah was eight months' pregnant and Vicky had a badge – a miniature version of herself – pinned to her top which I thought was really cool.

They'd make me do wrist exercises with the right hand, gentle exercises with my shattered left arm to prevent my muscles from getting weak, and lift my legs up to take the pressure off them. It sounds simple enough but after spending so long lying down, moulded into the bed sheets like a lump of clay, it felt strange and scary to be moving around. It reminded me how weak my body was, how it didn't feel like mine any more, as if my legs and arms were completely disengaged from my brain.

Some days when I heard the gentle squeaking of Vicky and Sarah's plimsolls coming towards my cubicle, I'd pretend to be asleep so I didn't have to face them.

Shortly after I had the second cast-boot fitted, Vicky and Sarah came and paid their usual visit.

'Shall we try and sit you up today?' Vicky said, smiling at me hopefully. But I was so weak and ill, my body as heavy as a bag of rocks, that the thought of trying to pull myself up seemed impossible.

'I just can't do it,' I said.

Undeterred, they returned in the afternoon, this time with Charlotte, a physio and lead trauma nurse. I knew I couldn't avoid them for a second time, and I didn't want to. In between their visits I'd received a fresh wave of beautiful cards and gifts, including a signed pink boxing glove from boxer Amir Khan. It was a fitting reminder that I had to keep fighting. So many

people were thinking of me. I couldn't let them down, I had be strong for their sake.

'So, shall we try sitting up again?' Charlotte asked.

Towering above me at nearly six feet tall, and with a no-nonsense demeanour, she wasn't the sort of person you said no to.

'OK, let's give it a go,' I replied, taking a deep breath.

They called in one more physio, so there were two on each side trying to help me up and support my neck. Slowly, very slowly, they inched me up. I felt like a rag doll, head lolling around from side to side. I slumped back on the pillows, the blood instantly whooshing from my head down my body, making me feel really dizzy, the room spinning as if I was being tossed around on the Waltzers at a fairground. I was feeling pretty frightened to be honest, but my family's claps and cheers at seeing me sit up took the edge off. And I'd done it! Something I'd taken for granted my whole life, but now realised how incredibly lucky I was to be able to do. Even if it did make me want to puke over my very kind audience, I could do it. It was progress.

'Can I be put down now, please?' I asked after a very long thirty seconds, breathing a sigh of relief as I was lowered back to my horizontal safe place.

Dad picked up one of the hundreds of cards we'd received and started to read it out. He barely managed to say the first line before he started to choke up on the words.

'Dad, get a grip,' I said, rolling my eyes.

A ripple of laughter floated around the ward as Dad sat there in a puddle.

'I'm sorry,' he sniffled, but as he said it, I also caught a little smile on the corner of his lips. I think it was always a relief for them to hear my re-surfaced cheek, a welcome sign that I was on the up.

Dad was on the night shift that evening. He'd nodded off in the chair but I couldn't sleep. I'd become paranoid that I'd roll on to my frame, jamming it into me, so most nights, in and amongst having these horrible hallucinations, I'd lie as still as possible, terrified of moving it. I went back to my old game – studying the ceiling – set to the new soundtrack of my life: the humming machines, the gentle 'slap slap' of the nurses' shoes as they did their circuit around the ward, the murmurs of the other patients. I hadn't met any of them, but I knew there were other young victims from the attack being treated just a few feet away, and I felt an inexplicable bond between us.

Suddenly, I sensed a tickly itch beginning to twitch right in the middle of my forehead. I tried waggling my eyebrows to get rid of it, but it didn't work.

'Dad, can you come and itch my head?' I called out.

Dad, half-asleep, made a grunting noise, shuffled to his feet and came over in a bit of zombie daze.

'Where is it itching?' he asked.

'Right in the middle of my forehead,' I replied.

Dad gave my head a little scratch, and then stumbled back into his chair again.

Just then the itch returned.

Argh.

I couldn't get poor Dad back up again, so I used all my strength to pull my arm up – which I wasn't really supposed to do – and used the splint over my right hand to get to the itch.

Oh my God. I can't describe to you how sublime it felt. Closing my eyes in bliss, I heard the sound of feet running toward me.

'Look at what she's doing!' Opening my eyes, I saw one of the nurses, Jess (famous for having the most flawless eyebrows I have ever seen) next to my bed, laughing.

'Freya's using her splint as a head scratcher!'

Dad, woken by the commotion, poked his head up from where he was lying beside my bed. I grinned at him.

'Look, Dad,' I said, showing off my new party trick.

'Wow!' he laughed, looking at me in amazement as if I'd just pulled off a dazzling circus act. 'Check you out! You'll have to show Mum when she comes in the morning.'

A week ago, the mere suggestion that I'd be able to make such a tiny movement had seemed impossible. I'd achieved two big small things in one day: sitting

up and scratching my head. They were definitely steps forward. And having Dad and the nurses celebrating with me in that moment, at this crazy hour of four o'clock in the morning, made it all the more special.

CHAPTER EIGHT
A Visitor

Though my head was fuzzy, I felt calm: a new sensation for me. Usually after surgery, as the effects of the anaesthetic wore off, I was left feeling scared and disorientated, my body trembling violently. Sometimes I'd start to scream; other times, I'd cry – big, fat tears blobbing on to my hospital gown.

But today was different – or perhaps I'd got used to it. After all, by now, I'd already had twenty-three hours of surgery, over five sessions, in eleven days, and I trusted the doctors and nurses who were looking after me implicitly.

'What are you talking about?' I mumbled to Mum and Dad.

Mum opened her mouth to speak, just as Georgia came running in, an excited smile flung across her face, long blonde hair flying around her shoulders.

'You're going to see Ariana Grande today!'

'What?!'

'I'm serious. You're actually going to see her. She's coming to the hospital.'

'What! What! Oh my God, I can't believe it!'

To say I was excited was an understatement. I was going to meet my idol – actually meet her. I looked at the clock, it was 7 p.m., on 2 June 2017. This time and date would be imprinted on my mind for ever.

My stomach flitted with butterflies as my mind jerked into overdrive, thinking of all the things I was going to say.

'I'm going to tell her about my favourite episode of *Victorious* and my favourite scene,' I babbled to Georgia. 'Oh, and her make-up. I have to ask her about her make-up. Her eyeliner is always so perfect. How does she do it?'

Nodding enthusiastically, Georgia, who's normally so cool and collected, joined in.

'And we've got to tell her about our favourite songs! What's that one you love again? Oh yeah, I remember . . . '

Georgia suddenly launched into 'One Last Time', looking at me as she sang the lyrics.

The rush of sadness came at me like a steam train. The last time I'd heard that song I was with Nell on the night of the concert – and I was instantly taken back to that moment.

I could picture us so clearly, the scene replaying in

my mind as if I were watching a film: we were standing up out of our seats high up in the upper tiers of the arena, gazing down at the stage below, where Ariana was standing. She wore a sweeping white hooded coat, white trousers and towering black strappy heels, her trademark glossy high ponytail swishing from side to side as she sashayed from the main stage down a narrow runway to a platform right in the audience. She seemed so close to her fans they could almost touch her.

'Imagine being down there,' I shouted into Nell's ear.

'I know, so cool!' she screamed back.

Not that we were complaining. Up here, like two birds perched high in the treetops, we had an amazing view over the whole arena. I'd been here before but was still in awe of the enormity of the space, rows upon rows of seats lined with people of all ages and backgrounds – families, friends, couples – united in their love of music, singing their hearts out, full of euphoria.

The arena was bathed in darkness with shards of blue and white light beaming out across the crowds and on to the platform, bouncing off Ariana's coat, casting her in a magical glow. All around, people's camera phones twinkled like fairy lights.

'One Last Time' started off slowly at first, Ariana walking up and down the platform, microphone close to her lips, her every movement, expression, beaming

out from the two huge screens floating on either side of the stage.

'Manchester, sing!' she said, and suddenly hundreds of voices joined in one, a sea of arms waving in the air.

As the track picked up pace, Ariana became lost in the moment, closing her eyes, her butter-soft vocals sending goosebumps running up my arms, Nell and I holding hands tightly, moved to tears by the sheer beauty of this moment as we belted out the words into the glimmering darkness, not a care in the world who was listening.

'Baba, I'm sorry, I'm sorry,' Georgia's worried voice cut through my memories.

I opened my eyes, my vision blurred from the silent tears streaming down my face and seeping into the neck of my hospital gown.

Since the day Dad had told me what had happened, this was the first time I'd really allowed myself to think about Nell. We'd been so happy in that moment, and, as the poignancy of Ariana's lyrics sunk in, there came a fresh wave of tears. *One Last Time*. It really had been the last time for all the innocent people who'd lost their lives that night.

As I sat there crying, I was vaguely aware of Dad running to the door and talking to someone. 'You have to be careful,' I heard him say. 'This is the first time Freya has got really upset about Nell.'

Then I saw the corner of her face, the iconic giant ponytail, and I became hysterical. I couldn't breathe, and my heartbeat monitor started racing, making lots of noise. (Top tip: Try to avoid being attached to a heart-rate monitor when you meet your idol – you will never look cool.)

All these nurses came running over. 'Breathe, just breathe,' they said, as I gasped for air.

After a few minutes, my chest settled, and then this tiny figure stepped forward, swamped in a huge green puffer jacket.

'Hi,' Ariana said with a smile, sitting down next to me.

Dad stood on the other side of the bed. 'When the attack happened, one of the first things Freya asked me was if you were OK,' he said.

'What?' she gasped, tears springing into her eyes, 'Never mind if I'm OK, I want to know if you're OK.'

We both sat together sobbing quietly, the pain and heartbreak of that night coming out with every tear.

'Nell would have loved to be here,' I said.

Ariana wiped her eyes, straightened in her seat and took hold of my hand. 'What are you talking about?' she smiled. 'Nell *is* here. She's saying "Oh my God! It's Ariana Grande!"'

I started to laugh as I pictured the look on Nell's face. That's *exactly* what she'd say.

Seeing me smile, Ariana started laughing too. I looked down at her hand with her perfect, long nails, and thought, 'Wow. Ariana Grande's hand is really on mine.'

She lay down a big, cuddly teddy bear and cheery yellow sunflower next to my bed. I noticed the yellow petals and green stem matched her yellow off-the-shoulder top and over-sized green jacket.

'These are for you,' she said, then, spotting my mum, she stood up and gave her a big hug.

'Hi, Mom!' she smiled, as Mum, only a smidge taller than Ariana, gave her a hug back.

Meanwhile, Georgia was scrolling through her phone.

'Look at this,' she said, beckoning Ariana over.

Ariana came and huddled around the phone, and then my face popped up on the screen, and my voice blared out, as a video started playing of me doing a rendition of one of Ariana's songs a couple of weeks before the concert.

I thought it'd be really funny to sing in a high-pitched tone, never in a million years thinking that the singer herself would actually listen to it.

'Oh no,' I cringed, sinking into the bedsheets. 'This is so embarrassing.'

'Wow, you can sing higher than me,' Ariana laughed. 'I love your whistle tone!'

I could feel my cheeks flushing red, but her perfectly

made-up face was full of smiles, and as she watched it she was looking back at me and beaming.

'Shall I take a picture?' Dad said.

'No,' I replied, instinctively. I suddenly felt really self-conscious. I knew I didn't look right. But then I instantly told myself off in my head.

Don't be silly. When will you ever get this chance again?

'OK, Dad,' I said. 'But a very quick one.'

Dad angled the phone towards us, took a couple of snaps, then started walking toward me, mobile outstretched, but I shook my head. I couldn't face myself, not yet.

Ariana took hold of my hand again.

'It was so special seeing you today. But I have to go now and visit Adam. Be strong, I love you, goodbye.'

Adam was someone else on the ward who'd also been injured in the attack – because the curtains were always shut around our beds, I never saw him.

As she turned to leave, Mum was hovering by the bed. She and Ariana looked at each other for a moment, then Mum's face went serious. 'Don't worry,' she said softly, 'it wasn't your fault.'

'Thank you, Mom,' Ariana replied, her voice quivering, turning around, her giant shiny high ponytail swishing around her, and giving me a wave.

I looked after her, and suddenly said to Dad, 'Wait, I really want her signature.'

Dad grabbed a notebook off the side and went running after her.

'Can you please write a signature for Freya?'

I saw her carefully writing something down, then Dad came over and showed me the page.

'Freya, I love you with all my heart, I'm so, so proud of you, stay strong my love, love always, Ariana Grande.'

It was such a beautiful note, my heart felt like it would burst.

Ariana's manager Scooter, who was hovering nearby, smiled when he saw how happy I looked at Ariana's message.

'I was in New York City when 9/11 happened,' he said. 'I thought the response from everyone then was amazing but it's nothing compared to Manchester. I'm completely in awe of you guys.

'You know, once Ariana got home after the concert, she called me in tears. She said, "I never want to sing again," but two or three days later she said, "I have to sing again for all those people, I have to go back." and that's when we organised the concert . . . '

Just then, Scooter was called away, and we waved him goodbye. Mum came and sat next to me and picked up the teddy bear and the sunflower. 'It's so brave of her to do the concert,' she said, stroking the bear's soft golden fur absentmindedly. 'She's so young herself, it must be so hard for her. I could tell

by the look in her face that she blames herself, but she shouldn't.'

I thought about Ariana, and how strong she was for returning to Manchester and putting on the One Love Concert. Her fighting spirit had filled me with hope and I thought, *If she can do it, so can I*. I fell asleep happy for the first time, a feeling which, if I'm to be honest, I never thought I'd properly feel again.

CHAPTER NINE
One Last Time

Seeing Ariana triggered memories of Nell, memories that I'd pushed far away, memories which were too painful to think about. The next day, Mum and Dad sat next to me and the emotions started tumbling out; the intense joy and love Nell and I had felt in the build-up to the concert and on the night.

After I'd given Nell the tickets, we plunged straight into what-are-we-going-to-wear mode. Here's the thing. When you go to a concert with your parents and sister, you don't really care what you're wearing. It's dark and you just fling on any old thing. But when you're with your friends . . . well, it's a different matter, isn't it? You have to look cool and make sure your outfit is Instagram and SnapChat-worthy.

Nell and I went shopping two weeks before the show for new clothes and make-up, spending two hours just

in Superdrug, swatching lipstick colours up our arms like tiger stripes.

'This colour would look great on you,' Nell said, picking up a coral pink and gliding it across my wrist.

I wrinkled my brow.

'I think it'd look better on you,' I replied.

I'd had a breakout of acne and wasn't feeling very confident about the way I looked, but Nell was so beautiful, inside and out. She could wear an old T-shirt and still look amazing.

In the end, I picked a red crop top, light-blue skinny jeans and a cherry-red lip to match, which felt incredibly grown-up for me. Nell, on the other hand, settled on a blush-pink one-shoulder ruffled top and denim shorts paired with smoky eye make-up. With her dark-rimmed glasses and shiny brunette hair, she looked the height of sophistication.

We spent every lunch break and hours on our phones after school planning every little detail from how we were going to do our hair (curls? beach waves? straight?) to travel plans and everything in-between.

The night before the concert, on Sunday 21 May, Nell called me on FaceTime as per usual.

'Do I look grown-up in this?' she asked, posing in her new outfit, hand on hip, adjusting the frills on her pink top.

'Yes!' I shouted enthusiastically. 'That looks great on you!'

She was coming over to mine straight after school on the Monday to get ready for the concert, so we ticked off all the things on her checklist to bring with her.

'Hair curlers?'

'Tick.'

'Make-up?'

'Tick.'

'Outfit?'

'Tick.'

'Handbag?'

'Tick.'

'Trainers?'

'Tick.'

Afterwards, I gave her a big smile.

'Happy Ariana Grande Eve!' I sang loudly, jiggling around and doing a little happy dance.

'Oh my God! I'm not going to be able to sleep!' she squealed back. Then in a flurry of goodbyes and 'I love you's, her smiley face flashed off the screen.

I beamed from ear to ear – Nell had always been the 'mum' in our friendship. I was so excited that for once I could repay the favour and take her somewhere she hadn't been before.

As I shut down my iPad, I had no idea that would be the last FaceTime chat we'd ever have.

CHAPTER TEN

Guilt

Guilt was starting to creep over everything like a mist. A large part of it was Nell: I kept torturing myself with thoughts that she'd only been at the concert because of me, and that I'd let her down, let her parents down. It wasn't fair that I was still here when she wasn't.

The other part was that I felt so guilty about what I was putting my family through. By the time my first week in the High Dependency Unit was nearly over, I could tell everyone was completely exhausted. There was Georgia, frantically running around between school and hospital, trying to sit her A levels, cramming in extra revision with a maths tutor because she'd fallen behind, and updating everyone on my progress behind the scenes; Mum, who'd taken it upon herself to look after me 24/7, only really taking a break when Dad forced her to get a snatched hour or two of rest over at Ronald McDonald House; and then Dad

himself, juggling shifts by my bedside with running his company in the power-generation business and relentlessly keeping everyone's spirits up with his contagious, and at times very dark, sense of humour.

As I took in the heavy bags under their bloodshot eyes, ash-grey complexions and unwashed hair, it made me feel like I was the lucky one here. I had all these people running around for me – I needed to hurry up and get better for them so that they could get back to some shred of normality.

But since Ariana's visit, the doctors had slowly begun reducing my painkillers, which meant I was physically starting to feel all the injuries I now had, and emotionally starting to feel the loss of Nell.

It was keeping me awake at night and, lying in bed left with these thoughts climbing over me that I was doing my best to escape from, I'd do anything to try and distract myself – and poor Mum was usually on the receiving end.

I'd end up calling out to her in the early hours for a sip of water from my Disney Princess cup, or to play an episode of my favourite show, *Gavin and Stacey*, on this little portable DVD player the hospital had loaned me.

After a couple of nights of this, Mum had got to the point of total exhaustion and, for the first time, said that she'd be leaving me to pop over to Ronald McDonald House to get some sleep. I felt scared, being

left on my own, in the darkness, with only the inside of my whirring mind for company.

'But I don't want you to go, Mum,' I said when she first told me. 'What if I need something?'

'Don't worry,' she said, stifling a yawn, her red, tired eyes filling up with guilt. 'Nurse Jenny is on the night shift and will look after you. I'm only across the road at Ronald McDonald House if you need me; they can ring the room and I'll come back straight away.'

I'd heard my parents talking about Jenny, telling me how lovely she was, but I'd always seemed to be in surgery when she was around and hadn't met her yet.

'OK,' I said, doing my best not to make a big deal out of it. 'Could you put *Gavin and Stacey* on for me before you leave?'

I watched Mum look through the pile of DVDs on the other side of the room and slot one into the player. As she kissed me goodbye, the Christmas Special pinged on, instantly making me smile as it was one of my favourite episodes.

The scene starts with the comedian James Corden, who plays the character Smithy, driving in his car singing his heart out to Band Aid's 'Do They Know It's Christmas?'.

The phone rings, and it's the main character, Gavin (played by Matthew Horne), and they both start singing it together.

'This is my favourite part,' I chuckled to myself.

Then I heard this singing floating across the bay.

'Let them know it's Christmas time!'

I looked up, and it was Jenny. With a nose ring, tattoos and lots of curly brown hair, she looked like a rock star. 'This is my favourite episode of *Gavin and Stacey*,' she said.

From that moment, I knew I liked her.

'You're up late,' she remarked, looking at her watch. 'It's 3 a.m.'

'I know, I'm having trouble sleeping,' I replied.

'What are you thinking about?' she asked.

'Nell,' I confided, sadly, my heart heavy.

Jenny gave me a smile, and pulled up a chair.

'Want to tell me what she was like?'

'OK,' I said, and before I knew it, a couple of hours had passed as I told Jenny how funny she was, how caring she was, how she looked so much older than me.

'I look around ten, and she looked eighteen,' I laughed. 'People couldn't believe we were the same age when they saw us together, she was always so much cooler than me.'

Despite only just meeting Jenny, I felt like I could tell her anything, which came as such a relief. Because although I knew I could always talk to my parents, I didn't want to upset them further, I didn't want my worries and fears keeping Mum awake at night, so it felt easier to talk to someone outside of the devastating situation we were in.

Jenny stayed with me until around 6 a.m., listening patiently, asking questions, and just . . . being there. It felt like a type of therapy, a tentative step in my healing process, though the wounds were still very raw.

It's funny, you think the longer you are in hospital, the better you will feel. But, to me, it seemed the opposite. As time went on, I continued to feel worse – physically and emotionally – as the pain from my injuries, and the pain from that night, intensified. After two weeks in hospital, the whiplash I'd suffered on my neck started to feel really sore, a tight stiffness running down my neck and seeping toward my shoulders and down my burned back. It made even the tiniest movements, like sipping water from a straw, excruciating. This made me feel guilty too, because, despite my injuries, I knew that I was lucky to be alive and to be under the care of so many amazing people.

I tried my best to put on a brave face and push forwards, but sometimes there were situations I had no control over which would put my family through hell. On 5 June, I was taken for more surgery to clean my wounds and change my dressings. As had become routine now, one moment I was drifting off to sleep as I went under, and the next I was blinking awake, small shards of light and movement drifting into view.

One shadow got larger, darker.

My eyes fluttered open.

'Jenny!' I exclaimed. Having bonded so quickly, I was so happy to see her. She started to cry, and as my eyes adjusted to the light in the room, I noticed that Mum, Dad and Georgia were all crying too. I was confused.

'What's happened?' I asked, throat raspy dry.

'We just feel happy, babe,' Mum replied, wiping away tears.

I'd come out of surgery a few hours earlier but had been refusing to wake up. Mum and Georgia had tried everything – from Georgia dancing around the ward singing 'Wakey wakey, Freya!' in various pitches, to Mum saying, 'It's time for school!' like a stern headteacher.

As the hours rolled by, they'd become increasingly worried about me, concerned that the emotional and physical pain I was starting to feel was taking its toll on my mental health, and that I was shutting down, escaping into a deep, cavernous sleep where no one could reach me.

I felt so bad that I'd made them worry about me, so I tried to be positive, and when the doctors said that my surgery had gone well, seeing the look of relief on Mum's face was a genuine lift.

I looked down at myself and was shocked to see that pretty much all of the dressings on my arms had been removed. 'I've been de-mummified!' I said to Mum and Georgia. It seemed strange to see my bare skin: my thin sausage-like arms were pale pink, red and mottled – but still there.

While I'd been in surgery, more beautiful cards had arrived. Once the doctors had gone and we'd all calmed down, Georgia positioned herself in the chair next to me as she always did and started to read them out, and I felt my foundations joining together again, like the parts of a toy racetrack neatly slotting into place. My chest felt warm and the lump in my throat resurfaced as it did every time we went through this ritual together. If the guilt was a mist, kindness was a sort of sunshine that made it retreat, if only for a little while. The love those cards contained was really beyond words, and I wished with all my heart that Nell, who had been so loving and caring herself, was here to see it.

CHAPTER ELEVEN

The Concert

When I woke up on the morning of 22 May, the first thing I did was reach over to my bedside table for my phone.

'Happy Ariana Concert Day!' I texted Nell.

'Oh my God, I'm so excited! I can't even explain to you! See you at school!' she replied back at lightning speed.

The moment I saw her in the playground, she came squealing up to me, her school bag bumping against her side.

'I can't believe we are actually doing this,' she said, the biggest smile on her face.

'Well, believe it!' I replied, feeling pleased with myself that I'd managed to give her such an amazing gift.

All day at school we chatted about Ariana, about her choreography and our favourite songs – 'Moonlight', a

slow ballad which shows off her vocals, and 'Greedy', all funky disco and great to dance to.

'But isn't it weird to dance at concerts?' Nell asked, forehead wrinkled.

'Once you're in the crowd, everyone just loses it,' I replied, assuming the air of a gig veteran. 'It's amazing.'

We had all our lessons together that day and the hours went by so slowly. I remember looking at the clock 24/7, barely being able to get any work done, tummy in constant butterflies.

In break times, we told anyone who'd listen that we were going to see Ariana Grande and as soon as the home-time bell rang, I grabbed Nell's hand and said, 'Let's go!'

Our friends Ellie and Annie gathered around to see us off. 'Have the best time!' they yelled as we waved our goodbyes and went running out of school.

Nell's mum was waiting around the corner so Nell could drop off her stuff. 'Hi,' she said, excitedly, slinging her school bag in the back of the car and giving her Mum a sweet smile.

'Muuuum, can I please have some money for merch?' she asked.

I giggled hearing her use the slang term for merchandise, thinking that I'd already trained her well.

'Do you really need it?' her mum asked.

'Oh yes, she does,' I chimed in, 'It's her first Ariana concert. She needs a souvenir.'

Nell's mum rummaged around in her purse.

'OK, here you go then,' she said, handing her a couple of notes.

'Thanks, Mum,' Nell replied, giving a hug and a kiss. 'I love you.'

'I love you too,' her mum replied. 'Have a great time. Bye!'

We went running down the street the thirty seconds it took to get to my house, racing up the path and flying through the front door. School finished at 3.30 p.m. and we were there by 3.40.

'Hi, Alison,' Nell said to my mum. 'How you doing?'

This always made me smile about Nell. She was really grown-up and talked to adults on their wavelength. I think that's why Mum liked her so much.

Georgia was sat in the living room, and the four of us chatted for a bit about a history assessment and how excited we were.

Nell showed my mum her outfit – 'What do you think, Alison?' 'Very nice, Nell,' – and then we thudded upstairs and started getting ready.

I was halfway through curling my hair and Nell was putting the finishing touches to her smoky eye make-up when we heard Mum yelling above Ariana's sweet vocals, 'Tea's ready!'

We went downstairs to find that Mum had laid out a special meal for us in the conservatory, with a giant pasta bake pride of place in the middle of the table.

'A treat for you girls,' she said, serving us huge portions. 'Got to keep your energy up for the concert.'

We sat and ate, Georgia joining us, laughing about stupid things that had happened that day, spitting out our pasta because we were giggling so much.

Then Mum came in – looking very pleased with herself, I must say – carrying a dish of warm homemade cookies and ice cream.

'This is incredible, Alison!' Nell said, polishing off her bowl, while I was so excited, I could barely eat anything.

After tea, we ran upstairs, put 'Dangerous Woman' back on, and sang along as we finished getting ready: we had to memorise the lyrics, it was more important than homework.

I was in the middle of doing my make-up when I noticed with a nervous pang that my curls were falling flat around my face. I glanced over at Nell, perfect curls bouncing around her shoulders.

'I can't do mine right, can you help me?' I asked.

She curled my hair, just like hers, and then she said, 'Would you like me to do some make-up?'

'Yes please!'

She sat me down on the bed with an air of authority. 'Right, we have five minutes, we can do this.' Leaning close to my face so that I could feel her breath tickling my nose, I was desperately trying not to laugh as she artfully applied my winged eyeliner and red lipstick.

Then, for the final flourish – a cat-ear headband. When I went to Ariana's concert in 2015, she was rocking a pair of black lace cat ears and I'd bought a pair to match.

'They look so cool!' Nell said as I placed them on my head. 'Ariana might see them!'

I slipped on a new pair of black leather lace-up boots with a tiny heel which made a clunking sound when I walked. They felt very grown up.

Nell stretched out her legs and put on her trainers.

'Aren't you going to be freezing?' I said as I eyed her denim shorts and ruffle one-shoulder bodysuit.

'Once we get dancing it will be hot!' she smiled.

'You're right – as usual,' I laughed, wondering if I should change out of my jeans. But there was no time. After two hours of getting ready, it was time to go. But first, a selfie. Nell and I went over to the window to get the best lighting, snapped a picture of each of us basked in a flattering sun-kissed glow, captioned them, 'Ariana Grande now x' and put them on SnapChat so everyone at school would see.

'Right, let's go!' I giggled, and we hurtled down the stairs. On hearing our excited footsteps, Mum and Georgia came to the front door to wave us off while my ever-ready Dad was already waiting for us in the car to drive us to the concert.

'Make sure Nell looks after the tickets and holds your hand so you don't get lost,' Mum said, biting her lip nervously.

'Don't worry, Mum,' I laughed.

'I know, but this is the first time you're going on your own, be careful.'

'Nothing's going to happen,' I said, grabbing hold of her hand, 'I'm not going to get lost, Nell is with me. She's literally like my mother, everything will be fine.'

Mum sighed. I could tell she was a little apprehensive, but she knew Nell was sensible. I don't think she would have let me go with anyone else.

'OK, have a great time! I'm so jealous. Love you,' Mum said giving us a hug and a kiss.

'I love you,' I sang back.

'Bye, Alison, thanks for tea,' Nell added.

We giggled to the car and, buckling up in the back seat, I turned to Nell, brandishing my phone.

'Selfie time!'

'I haven't even left the drive yet!' Dad laughed, rolling his eyes at us in the rear-view mirror.

I adjusted my hair and tried to pull my best pout. With her eyes shut and blowing a kiss toward the camera, Nell looked really cool while I had an awful duck face. Still, on Snapchat it went.

'Now for "Dangerous Woman",' I squealed, clicking the play button on my phone, and suddenly Ariana boomed into the car and we started screaming the lyrics out.

Along the way, Dad started asking Nell about school. We were picking our options for GCSEs around that

time and Nell thought she might like to be either a psychiatrist or a physiotherapist, so wanted to take Psychology (we all had to do science), along with RE and Drama. The latter are my favourite subjects, so it meant we would be in lessons together.

By the time we got off the motorway into Manchester, I was already losing my voice. It was warm that evening, so we had the windows down, music up loud. There was a Deliveroo driver cycling along next to us, and as we stopped at the traffic lights, I screamed at him: 'We're going to see Ariana Grande!'

He looked at us bemused while Nell and Dad burst out laughing. By now, the Arena wasn't far off, and Dad was giving Nell instructions. 'You have to take the tickets . . . Freya, let me see you give Nell the tickets . . . So you know where to go? . . .'

Dad pulled up just around the side of the Arena, about 200 metres away from the entrance.

Turning to us, he said, 'OK, do you know everything you are doing? Remember to text me when the concert is finished and you're ready to be picked up. I'll be just next door at the train station if you need anything . . . '

'Dad, we are absolutely fine,' I replied, sliding out of the car, and even though the Arena was right in front of me, I started walking in the opposite direction.

Dad wound down the window. 'That's the wrong way! That gives me no hope whatsoever!'

Nell took my arm.

'Come on, it's this way,' she giggled.

We all laughed, as Dad hung out the car window.

'Love you, Dad,' I said.

'Have fun, girls,' he yelled.

I looked back at him a couple of times, waving and shouting, 'Bye, Dad!' as he waited in the car to check we got in safely.

As Nell and I walked up the steps into the Arena, I gripped her tightly, my stomach knotted with nerves with the responsibility of looking after my best friend.

CHAPTER TWELVE
Hair

I was back to my game of staring up at the ceiling, Mum was sitting next to me, reading, when I suddenly had a vision of cat ears.

'Mum,' I said. 'When the explosion happened, I was lying on the floor and out of the corner of my eye, I could see these dangling cat ears.'

Mum's chest rose anxiously.

'They'd melted into your head,' she said, quietly. 'And so had the plastic backpack you'd been wearing. That's why we've been finding it so difficult to brush your hair.'

My mind darted back to the sports bag. Before the concert started, Nell and I had gone off to the merchandise stand in the foyer of the arena, and she'd helped me pick out a hot-pink Ariana T-shirt.

'Let's get these as well,' I'd said, pointing at matching hot-pink wristbands. Giggling, we wriggled the bands

over our hands, while the guy at the stand popped my T-shirt into a black drawstring plastic bag.

I looped the strings over my shoulders so the bag bobbed on my back as Nell and I linked arms and ran off toward to the doors leading into the Arena. We were so excited that we were nearly tripping over ourselves.

Flash-forward to after the attack happened. I saw myself lying on the floor of the train station, paramedics hunched over me, metal glinting. What I didn't realise at the time was that they were using a pair of scissors to try and cut the bag out of me because the plastic was seeping and melting into my hair, the drawstring stuck in my arm like a piece of cheese wire slicing through a wedge of cheddar at a supermarket deli counter.

'We tried to wash your hair while you were unconscious in ICU,' Mum's voice brought me back into the room. 'Every time I kissed you, all I could smell was burning. It was upsetting Dad too and we were desperate to get rid of the smell. But it was impossible.' She said even now my hair was dirty, that it was knotted with lumps of plastic and shrapnel. 'It might need to be cut off.'

My eyes instantly watered. 'Mum, please. I don't want my hair cut off.'

I know it sounds silly, but in that moment, out of all my injuries, this upset me the most because I loved my hair. To a teenage girl, hair is everything.

When I was younger, it was chin-length, cut in a bob, a pale-blonde wispy halo framing chubby cheeks. But, after I started high school, I started growing it, looking after it, brushing it, conditioning it, and as a result, my hair had become thicker and shinier. By the time the concert came around, it was my crowning glory, a swingy blonde sheet. Every morning before school I'd style it differently; high ponytail, French plait, pigtails, fishtail side plait. Now, laying here helplessly, I couldn't even brush it. It felt matted and dirty around my neck, leaving a trail of grimy oiliness on my skin. I'd do anything to have it washed. Then, something amazing happened. One of the ward sisters, Emma, said that she'd arranged for a couple of her hairdresser friends, Simon and Karen, to come in and sort my hair out for me. I was so touched, and incredibly thankful.

I knew that when the hairdressers came, I'd need to get myself out of the bed and sit in the big blue armchair tucked in the corner of the room to give them easy access to my head.

It would be a challenge – up until then, I'd only managed to sit up in bed – but washing my hair was such a run-of-the-mill thing to do. In my mind I had to do it to prove to myself that I still could. So, the day before the hairdressers were due to come in, with the help of my physio, I set myself the goal of sitting up with my legs dangling off the side of the bed.

I took a deep breath, and used all my strength to hoist myself up and over, battling against the frame on my right arm and heavy boots weighing me down.

'Freya, you did it!'

Mum, who's normally incredibly softly spoken, jumped up from her seat, whooping and clapping as if she'd just won the lottery.

'Go, Freya!' Georgia shrieked.

As my family cheered me on, I gave a faint smile, but in my head I thought, *I feel so sick.*

The room was spinning again, and my stomach was in knots. I had a bucket next to me, and I kept glancing at it, thinking, 'I'm going to puke.'

After a few moments, the physio eased me back down onto the bed and I'd never been so relieved to be lying down. Staring at the ceiling, I willed my stomach to settle. No matter how much pain I was in, I knew I'd have to attempt it again the next afternoon for my hairdressing session.

When the time came, I took a deep breath and managed to sit on the edge of the bed again. The physios had wheeled in a hoist to help transport me from the bed to the armchair. It looked like those huge trollies you find in DIY stores to carry heavy goods and took up most of the space in the cubicle.

The hoist went underneath me and then lifted me up; as it moved, my frame was squashed into my side. I screamed out in pain.

'I know it hurts but you need to breathe through it,' the nurse said.

They gave me extra painkillers and I screamed all the way until they eased me down into the big blue armchair. It was the first time sitting in anything which wasn't my bed, and was so uncomfortable my body seemed to collapse in on itself like a deflated balloon, reminding me of how injured I was.

My mum came and sat on the bed opposite me.

'I know that was hard, but look at you! You're sat up! You should feel so proud of yourself!'

I looked at her smiling face, and tried to breathe through my pain like the nurse had told me to.

Just then, the hairdressers came in.

'Hi, Freya, we're going to try and sort out your hair, is that OK?'

'Yes!' I replied, smiling in relief.

It took an hour of brushing and untangling before they managed to run a comb through it.

'How you are managing to sit there for so long, I don't know,' Mum said, wincing as they tugged at my hair.

But I didn't care if I broke another bone doing it, I knew it would feel so good to have my hair washed.

Eventually, they managed to untangle it and wash out most of the muck, but there was still a small section at the back which was extremely damaged.

'We'll have to cut it out,' they said.

I was apprehensive, but they reassured me that it wouldn't be noticeable and, after two hours, they had finally finished.

Dad took a photograph of the back of my head for me, and when he showed me the picture, I couldn't believe it. Shiny, glossy, golden – my hair looked like something out of an advert.

'Thank you so much,' I said, welling up at the hairdressers' generosity and kindness. 'You don't know how much this means to me.'

Before they left, they styled it in two Heidi-like plaits so it would be easy to manage. I could just about reach with my right hand and stroke them, making me feel so much better. It was a style I often did for school, and back in bed, I started to think about my friends. I felt so guilty that I wasn't there to comfort them and suddenly had an idea.

'I want to let school know that I'm OK,' I said to Dad as he sat with his legs crossed in the chair next to me. 'Maybe I should go and do a speech in assembly?'

Dad looked surprised.

'When we get there, we can think about it,' he replied.

'I will get there, I want to do that,' I said, determined.

As the day went on, thoughts continued to swirl about how my friends must be feeling about the attack, how heartbroken they must be about Nell and worried about me here in hospital. For the first time, I started to feel anger towards the suicide bomber for doing this

to us and suddenly had an overwhelming desperation to see his face, to see the man who had caused so much devastation.

'I want to see him, I want to see the bomber,' I said to Dad.

Dad, Mum and Georgia all looked at me, faces turning milk-pale.

'I don't think that's such a good idea,' Dad replied.

'Dad, I think I need to see it.'

Dad hesitated, as if he were battling in his own head about what he should do. Then he started scrolling through his phone.

He stared at the screen for a few moments, then pointed it toward me.

When I saw the image, I felt instantly shocked.

I was transported back to the night of the concert as my consciousness was flooded with fresh memories.

After the gig had finished, Nell and I were in the foyer, walking towards the train station . . . She had gone to put her drinks cup in the bin . . . I'd got out my phone to type Dad a message and saw this guy stood in the centre of the foyer, dressed all in black, glasses, a baseball cap . . .

It was the man in the photo.

'I saw him,' I said, quietly, my voice trembling. 'I saw him.'

CHAPTER THIRTEEN

The Antidote to Anger

I stirred, softly, murmuring. A distant beeping became nearer, louder as the blanket of sleep pulled away, exposing me to reality, to the hospital, to the noises which had nudged me awake over the last three weeks.

I tried to open my eyes, but this time they were painful, stinging, shrouded in darkness. Wincing, I managed to peel open my left eye, and peered through a small chink in my lashes. I instantly knew that I was in a different place. The ceiling looked different, not so cracked. Smooth, shiny, white. In fact, it was quite nice as far as ceilings go.

'I can't open my eye,' I croaked through my sand-paper throat.

'It's OK,' Mum replied. 'You've been in surgery and have a patch over your left eye. Just rest, gorgeous. It's OK.'

The now familiar post-op fog started to clear and the pain in my left eye became more acute. It felt swollen and sore, as if someone had been poking around in there.

Through my good right eye, I took in my surroundings.

The walls were white and clinical, the cubicle was stark and sterile, it was quiet, eerily quiet, a complete contrast to the hustle and bustle of the HDU with its natural light flooding through my window and shining on to my bed.

'Where am I?' I said.

'You're in the Burns Unit. It's very . . . ' Mum paused, 'different here, isn't it?'

Mum explained there were rules to being in Burns. Due to an increased risk of infection, everything had to be kept super clean and I wasn't allowed any visitors apart from my immediate family. My heart sank. I liked having visitors. Hearing about normal day-to-day things reminded me that there was a life outside of hospitals and operations and burns and dressings.

Without them, it would feel like I was stuck in this clinical world indefinitely.

I closed my eyes, a sadness sliding over me as my thoughts flitted between Nell, the bomber's face, my injuries, back and forth like a terrified moth caught in a lampshade.

'I'm just going to keep my eyes closed for a while,' I called out to Mum, hoping I could shut out the pain I was feeling.

'OK, love,' she replied, squeezing my right arm gently, her voice tinged with worry.

I don't know how long I was lying there, but a doctor's voice caught my attention.

'I have good news,' he said. 'The operation to remove the shrapnel from Freya's eye has been a success. Her eye is now clear and her wounds are healing really well.'

I heard Mum gasp, then let out a sob.

'She's not scheduled for any more surgery at the moment,' the doctor continued. 'We'll have to remove the external fixator from her left arm, but that will be later on down the line.'

At those words, I opened my left eye, peered at the doctor, then to Mum as she burst into tears, her shoulders shuddering as if she were shaking off all the uncertainty, the worry, the waiting which had piled on to her with each operation.

The last time I'd seen her this emotional was on the night of the attack, just before I was wheeled off for the first of my many surgeries. Since then, she'd been trying so hard to hold it together, to be our rock, but knowing that I wouldn't have to face any more operations for the time being was overwhelming.

'I can't believe it,' she cried, wiping her eyes with an ancient tissue she'd found stuffed in her pocket, flakes of paper fluttering on to her trousers. 'Thank you, thank you.'

As Mum chatted with the doctor, I managed a small smile, but inside a storm of sadness which had been threatening for so long had begun. I couldn't stop thinking about the attack and all the pain and suffering which had been caused. What's going on in the world where people want to do this to one another?

It was all just too much. Too much.

The next day, I still couldn't bear to open my eyes. Not just because they were sore, but because I just wanted to block everything out. Though my surgeries were finished for now, a long road to recovery lay ahead. I'd been in hospital for three weeks, and the most I'd managed to move this destroyed body of mine on my own was lifting up my right arm to scratch my head and shuffling to the edge of the bed. Something as simple as washing myself was now in the hands of the nurses who came in every day to give me a bed bath and keep me clean with wet wipes. Along with the physio, it was the worst time of day as it hurt, and I felt incredibly self-conscious, especially as a teenager whose body had started changing. I lay there, feeling so helpless and weak – not helped by the fact that I'd completely lost my appetite, partly due to the combination of the drugs I was on, but also the injuries I'd sustained to my teeth, jaw and mouth. The whole area felt so fragile that so far I'd only managed to suck on food which instantly turned to mush, like strawberries and Quavers. I've always been slight – 5 foot 3 inches

and around 45 kilos – but I'd lost so much weight that I felt like a shell, and no matter how much my parents tried to get me to eat, I just couldn't stomach anything.

For the first time, I really wanted to go home. But when was I ever going to get out of here? It seemed never-ending. And with the Burns Unit being so unnervingly subdued, with no real distractions to plaster over my seeping thoughts or chats with nurse Jenny, who I'd left behind in the HDU, I had the head space to think about what had happened.

I felt so angry at the bomber for doing this to me, I felt angry at the bomber for taking Nell away, I felt angry at the bomber for causing my family so much pain, I felt angry at the bomber for devastating the lives of so many people.

As I lay there, with all this turmoil going on in my head like clothes in a tumble dryer, I heard the tap, tap, tap of Dad's fingers flying over his laptop keyboard.

Back in the HDU, I'd noticed Dad would often be sitting in the chair in the corner of the room on his evening shift and be typing away. I assumed he was doing work and in the back of my head I'd thought, 'Oh, thanks, Dad.'

So, when I actually found out what he was doing, it came as a shock.

'Right, Freya,' he said, 'I'm going to put on the blog tonight that you're not doing well today.'

My eyes crept open and I looked at him, confused.

'What blog?' I said.

'We've been writing a blog to keep everyone updated on your progress,' he said. 'We've been posting twice a day.'

I listened, taken aback, as Dad explained that when I first arrived in hospital, his phone was going mad with people calling and messaging to find out how I was. He found himself constantly darting out into the corridor to the only spot next to a large window where he could find any decent phone reception, and Mum had started getting upset that he kept leaving us. So, he asked the school whether he could start a blog on their website to keep everyone updated and it had grown bigger and bigger.

'People were reading it, and asking what they could do to help,' Dad continued. 'So, I started a JustGiving page to raise money for the hospital. It's been crazy. People have been getting in touch from all around the world – New York, Germany – with words of support and donations. It's been unbelievable, really kept us going.'

'From around the world?' I muttered in disbelief.

I think that was one of the first moments that I really realised the scale of the attack and the impact it had had.

'Do you want me to read you today's post?' Dad asked.

I nodded, not really knowing what to expect.

He'd written about how after the euphoria of last night's news about not having any more surgery, I'd been very quiet today. He said he'd realised that I couldn't bear to hear any pop music, even in the background.

Music is such a big part of her life that we hope she can learn to love it again.

'How does that sound?' Dad asked, looking at me expectantly.

'OK,' I replied quietly.

I was so taken aback that I didn't really know what to say. Even though my family were with me every day, it still felt strange to hear what it was like from their perspective.

His concerns about the music played on my mind. I thought about that very first Miley Cyrus concert Mum and Dad had taken us to when Georgia and I were little and how special it had been. I felt sad that something which had brought us so much happiness could now cause so much pain.

A turbulent night followed as I got swallowed up in a dark hole of despair. It was the first time that I'd felt sorry for myself. I hated feeling that way because I still so desperately wanted to be positive for everyone around me. But in that moment I felt like the unluckiest person in the world. I was engulfed with fear, worrying that I wasn't going to get any better and just couldn't shake the thought from my head. I felt really guilty, convinced that Nell's mum must hate me because I

had survived, and Nell hadn't. Over and over it went in my head – that moment when we'd said goodbye to her, two of us going off to the concert, only one of us coming back alive. I was the one who had given her the ticket. I wished it was me who had died and not my beautiful, funny, sweet friend.

By morning, I was at my lowest ebb. I didn't feel like talking or seeing anyone. I just wanted to be left alone.

'How are you feeling today?' Mum asked, walking in from a night at the Ronald McDonald House with Dad and Georgia. I pointed at the emoji board that my acting teachers Jenny and Lee had brought me when I was in the HDU. It had different emojis on flip cards to express how I was feeling without having to say.

Flipping through slowly with my right hand, I chose a crying face, an angry face, a broken heart and 'zzz'. Four pictures which summed up how wretched I was feeling.

My parents and sister exchanged glances, silently agreeing that it was probably best to give me space and let me rest for a while.

Along with the emoji board, Jenny and Lee had also given me a beautiful silver bangle with the quote etched into the surface: 'She believed she could, so she did.' At the time I'd been so inspired by the words but now, as I lay in a pit of hopelessness and despair, that sliver of positivity seemed to have floated far, far away.

As the morning went on, I became lost in memories about Nell, tears trickling down my cheeks. Finally, I couldn't keep it in any longer.

'I miss Nell,' I cried out. Mum, Dad and Georgia turned to look at me, their faces crumpling with sadness.

'I know, Baba,' Georgia said, stroking my hair. 'I really miss Nell too.' As we sat there lost in our thoughts, I suddenly remembered a funny thing that had happened when we went shopping a couple of weeks before the concert and found myself telling Georgia the story.

Nell had got carried away in Superdrug and went to the till with a basket heaving with make-up. As the cashier rung through each item, we stood there, chatting excitedly about the night, not really paying much attention to the rising bill pinging up on the screen. Then, the cashier said, 'That'll be £70, please,' and Nell's mouth fell open in shock. 'I, er, didn't realise it'd be that much,' she stammered, her cheeks growing rose-red in embarrassment, and I collapsed into quiet hysterics as she sheepishly put back half the items, shrieking 'Freya!' at me. It was such a small but happy memory, blighted by sadness at the realisation that we'd never be able to make any more. I knew my injuries would heal in time, but I also knew the pain of losing Nell would be the slowest to heal, if it ever did.

After I'd chatted to my family about her, I felt drained but a little better. I hadn't wanted to burden them with

how sad I was feeling, but it was a comfort to talk about her and to remember how special our friendship was.

Georgia looked at me, her face brightening.

'I know,' she said, looking around at the cold, sterile cubicle, 'why don't we decorate this place a bit, put some cards and photos up?'

'OK,' I replied with a small smile.

So, we sat together, going through some of my favourite giant cards, and photos we'd taken on family holidays to America, and then Georgia stuck them up, on the walls and the monitor, a constant reminder of all the love and support that existed for us.

As I gazed at them, my mind went back to what Dad had told me about the blog. It hadn't really sunk in at the time, but now, faced with all these beautiful cards and messages, it started to hit me just *how many* people were cheering me on.

I gave myself a mental shake.

'Right, let's do this, Freya Lewis,' I told myself. 'Let's get better for all these people.'

Later on that afternoon, Dad asked if I'd like to watch something on my portable DVD player, and Georgia suggested one of our favourite childhood films, *High School Musical*.

We'd watched it so many times when we were little, my heart sang thinking about it.

'Sounds fun,' I replied, 'and . . . I think I want to watch it in the chair.'

I hadn't sat in the chair again since having my hair done, but I knew that if I wanted to get better for everyone, then I had to start moving – no more pretending to be asleep during physio sessions.

So, when Vicky came by a bit later, I told her I'd like to go in the chair.

'OK!' came her enthusiastic reply, and she went off to get the DIY-style trolley to help me. Vicky positioned it at the end of the bed, then helped me to sit up with my feet dangling off the edge, before I managed to stand on the trolley. Then I was wheeled the couple of feet to the chair, and she helped me sit down. As my body crumpled into the hard leather, I felt so uncomfortable, but I knew I had it in me to withstand it.

'You can do this, Freya,' I told myself.

Meanwhile, Georgia got the DVD ready, and the moment the film started playing, I was transported to my happy place, a childhood full of laughter, films, family time, holidays – and music. I'd been scared that every time I listened to music, I'd instantly be taken back to the night of the attack, but hearing the songs I'd grown up with reminded me that music could bring back wonderful memories too. For two hours, I got lost in this magical world, and afterwards, although my neck felt stiff and sore, my heart was lifted.

'Let's listen to more songs,' I said to Georgia.

'Are you sure?' she asked tentatively, knowing how upset I'd become when she'd started to sing Ariana's 'One Last Time'.

'Yep, I'm sure,' I replied. 'I've missed it.'

It still astounds me how such a little thing like watching a film could make such a big difference to my state of mind.

Feeling stronger, I gave myself my second pep talk of the day.

'Right, stop being silly,' I said to myself. 'You shouldn't have thought any of that stuff about how unlucky you are.'

Because, the fact is, if I thought like that, then it meant the terrorist would have won. And I was determined: I wasn't going to let him rob any light from my life.

PART TWO

PART TWO

CHAPTER FOURTEEN
Start Talking

Back in the HDU, a couple of psychologists had visited me to see if I wanted to talk about the attack. At the time, I hadn't felt ready to discuss it with anyone other than my family: the memories were too fragmented, raw, painful. But now I realised that if I really wanted to move forward – get stronger, get better – I needed to open up.

'OK, Freya, well, we'll leave you to it then,' Mum said, a slight tremble in her voice as she steadied herself on Dad's arm and headed out of the door to sit in the corridor.

The two therapists positioned themselves in high-backed red chairs next to my bed. As soon as I saw them, I instantly felt at ease as they both looked so unthreatening; Sonia was tiny and Daniel had a wide, friendly smile. Sonia swept a strand of her long black hair out of her eyes as she placed a box of tissues and

a jug of water on the side table next to my bed, while Daniel smiled at me through his glasses.

'Freya, start at a point where you feel comfortable.'

And with those words, everything I remembered came pouring out.

Nell and I went up what felt like the million steps to the Arena and when we reached the top, there was a bag check.

We stood in the queue, looking at people's outfits.

'I don't like her trousers.'

'No, I don't like them either . . . '

The line shuffling forward, we opened our small shoulder bags ready for the check – I had money and my glasses in mine, Nell had the money her mum had given her and the all-important tickets in hers.

With a swift once-over, we were waved in.

'Right, toilets,' I said to Nell, knowing that we should grab our chance now, before the concert started. After I'd finished, I waited for Nell outside, adjusting my cat ears when they got stuck in my beautifully styled curls. I was tussling with them, growing increasingly flustered, when Nell sprung up beside me. 'What's going on here?' she laughed, helping me untangle myself. With cat ears safely in place, we went to the merchandise stall, where I bought the Ariana T-shirt and we got matching pink wristbands, and then we excitedly went off to find our block – 205 – in the upper tiers of the Arena.

We excitedly walked through the doors into the concert hall, and were instantly plunged into darkness as the support act had already started.

'Can you tell us where these seats are?' we asked a woman with a bib and a torch, showing her our tickets. 'Over there,' she said, shining the light high up the stairs to our seats.

Nell grabbed hold of me, and we awkwardly went up the stairs, stepping over people, to get to our spot.

Finally settling into our seats, we turned our attention to the singer on stage – Victoria Monet. I'd never heard of her before but she sounded like Beyoncé: full of energy, sass and cool dance moves.

I texted Dad, swaying to the rhythm.

'We're sat in our seats and the support act is amazing!'

His reply pinged back. 'Oh really? Wow!'

After she'd finished, the other support act, BIA, started, but she wasn't our cup of tea so we decided to go and get a drink before Ariana came on.

We climbed down all the steps again, me holding on to the back of Nell so I didn't fall over, and we stood in a giant queue to get Nell a Sprite.

'I'm getting a large one in case you want some,' she said.

I remember thinking that's so sweet – but then that was Nell through and through, always thinking of others.

Clasping her big cup, we started walking back, when I suddenly realised that I'd left our tickets under our seats.

'What if security doesn't let us in?' I panicked, almost in tears.

'Don't worry, it'll be OK,' Nell replied, and just as she predicted, the guards just let us in. By the time we'd stumbled back to our seats in the dark, there was still forty-five minutes to go until Ariana came on stage. To fill the time, we started playing our favourite game at school.

'OK, so give me boys in our year to rate out of ten,' Nell said, and we sat there giggling for around twenty minutes as I chucked various names at her. After we'd tired of that, we tried messaging a few girls in our year who were also at the concert, but the signal in the Arena was awful.

'I wonder how long until Ariana comes on?' I said to Nell, and suddenly everything went black and a big countdown flashed up on the screen with only ten minutes to go. A mock-up of Ariana getting ready for the concert started playing, and as soon as we saw her, we started screaming.

With every single minute that passed, we looked at each other, shouting:

'Nine minutes!'
'Eight minutes!'
'Seven minutes!'

The suspense in the air was electrifying and I could feel my heart galloping away.

'I'm hyperventilating,' I laughed at Nell, melodramatically putting my hand to my chest.

'I know,' she replied, her cheeks flushed, 'I can't believe the actual Ariana Grande is going to be stood there!'

'We have to calm down, calm down.'

Just as I said it, the Arena vibrated with the unified voice of hundreds of people counting down the final minute and we were overcome with excitement.

'Give me your hand,' I said to Nell, mine outstretched. She held my hand tightly and we just sat there in anticipation. When the countdown got to zero, the music started playing and Ariana walked on to the stage.

Nell burst into tears.

'Don't cry,' I said, squeezing her hand.

The first song was 'Be Alright', and we stood up, screaming the lyrics, trying to dance in the narrow space between the seats and the barrier of our row.

After the first couple of songs, Ariana stopped and said: 'Hey, Manchester!' and we both looked at one another, our faces glowing with happiness, screaming, 'She's so nice!'

I flashed up the playlist on my phone so we could see which song was coming next.

'Shall we sit down?' I said, my legs beginning to ache. 'I'm exhausted!'

'Don't you dare sit down!' Nell laughed back.

So we stood there, linking arms, getting fifty million Snapchat videos, singing all the songs.

On came Nell's favourite – 'Touch It' – where Ariana repeats the lyrics, 'touch it, touch it'. Every time she said it, Nell prodded me in the arm, making us dissolve into fits of hysterics.

Finally it got to 'Dangerous Woman'.

'This is the last song,' Ariana said.

Nell looked at me, crestfallen. 'I don't want it to be the last song, I don't want to leave.'

'I know, neither do I.'

Nell grabbed hold of my hand, and pulled me into her; her top felt damp from all the dancing, and I was hot and sweaty too, but we didn't care. We screamed out the lyrics of 'Dangerous Woman', really going for it, as if it was the last song we'd ever sing.

'I love you!' Nell said.

'I love you too!' I replied.

'This is incredible, I'm going to remember it for ever, I can't wait to tell everyone tomorrow.'

Then, towards the end of the song, a shower of bright, fluorescent balloons floated down on the stage, and it seemed like such a magical end to a truly magical night.

I didn't want to leave, but Dad's words rung in my ears about getting out of the concert early to try and beat the crowds.

'Dad told us to get up really quickly,' I said to Nell.

'Right, take my hand,' Nell replied, and started leading me through the throng of people. As I looked around, I found it a bit weird because usually at concerts around that time, everyone starts to leave, but it was just us and a few others making an exit, despite it being only minutes before the concert finished.

I held on to Nell as she led me down the steps in the pitch black, towards the exit, and we made it to the main foyer. We were meeting Dad at the train station, but as I looked around, I was confused. 'I don't know where we're going,' I said.

Nell looked up and pointed. 'That sign says "train station". Let's go that way.'

We followed the direction of the sign and, along the way, Nell spotted a bin, so went to throw away her empty cup of giant Sprite. In the meantime, I got my phone out and typed out a message to Dad.

'We're on our way!! Xx.'

I was about to press 'send', when I looked up and saw this guy. He was stood in the centre of the main foyer around ten metres away from me. He was dressed all in black with a black cap and glasses with a backpack. He was facing towards me, looking straight forward. I could see the side of his face and thought it was a bit strange as he just had this deadpan expression. I only looked at him for a couple of seconds, before Nell came back.

'You ready?' she said.

'Yes!' I replied.

She put her stuff back in her bag and then looked at me with a big smile.

'That was the best night of my entire life,' she said.

'Really?' I beamed, 'I'm so glad.'

She linked arms with mine, just like we always did in school, so we were really close, and said, 'Right, let's go.'

As we walked along, the foyer was beginning to fill up with people.

'I love you more than anything in the world,' she said.

'I love you too,' I replied, smiling.

I was still clutching my phone in my hand, yet to send the message to Dad. I looked down, pressed 'send', and in that exact moment, everything went wrong.

There was a piercing sound – the loudest thing I'd ever heard – and I was flown forward into a giant bright light. It was like in films where people are blasted into the air by the sheer force of something.

As I was falling forwards, everything felt like it was happening in slow motion. I could feel Nell's arm slipping out of my mine, and the next thing I remember is being face-down on the floor.

I raised my head and I couldn't see anything, everything was black. I went to push myself up, but it didn't feel right. I don't know how long it took me, but I finally managed to get on my feet. In my muffled head, I assumed Nell was right behind me, so I tried to push

myself forward, thinking I was leading the way for both of us. Only I felt completely numb and there was a huge weight on my arm pulling me down. I looked at my left shoulder, and I could just make out my whole bone as my arm hung off my body. Dark patches were blooming all down my clothes, and although I couldn't see clearly I could sense that it was blood, lots of blood.

A high-pitched noise rung in my ears like a continuous car alarm was going off inside my head. It was dark; I looked into the shadows and could see smudgy silhouettes of people standing, and also some large objects on the ground – in hindsight, I know those objects must have been people, but at the time I couldn't process that.

The lights came back on and I tried to call out 'Help me' but the words wouldn't come out right; everything felt numb, my speech completely jumbled. In my head I thought, *This is so weird, why is no one coming to help?* And then I saw people running past me and, confused, I told myself, 'If people are running past me, how come I'm just stood here?' So, I tried to walk, but my legs felt really weak. I looked down and saw my jeans were ripped open and that they were covered in blood. I stumbled forward, nothing feeling right, and looked around at everyone, saying, 'Help me, help me.'

Then, this woman, who was closest to me, looked directly at me. I noticed she had dangly earrings on, hair up in a fancy do, face filled with horror.

As soon as I saw her, it was as if a dam suddenly disappeared inside me and pain flooded forwards. I fell, collapsing into her arms. She screamed as we both staggered to the floor, with me on top of her.

I lay on her chest, as she struggled to hold me up.

I was slipping as she cried and trembled.

'Phil!' she shrieked urgently.

A man came running over and looked at me.

'Kim? What happened?'

Kim started wailing, her face white, as I stared up at the ceiling, confused. I focused my gaze up ahead because I knew if I looked at anything else, my arm, my legs, the blood, I'd start to panic. My vision was really blurry, my hair was over my face and my arm was in excruciating pain, as if someone were stabbing me. I was screaming, though it felt like the noise was coming from someone else.

'What's wrong?' Kim asked me.

'My arm, my arm,' I replied.

'Phil, give her your jacket,' she said.

He pressed it down onto my arm, and in that moment, a chill came over me and I started shaking uncontrollably.

The screeching in my ears had pared back slightly, and I could just about hear all these alarms going off. A voice said over and over, 'Please exit the Arena now, please exit the Arena now.' Out of the corners of my eyes I could see the railings of the balcony which

overlooked the train station platform, so I remember thinking, 'OK, I'm at the station now.'

I had a sudden thought of *Is this a dream?* but dismissed it: *No, I was with Nell a moment ago.*

I tried to say her name, but it just came out as a noise.

'What?' came a voice. 'Who are you here with?'

As soon as I managed to say 'My friend', I lost it. I couldn't cry as I was in such shock and pain, so I lay there, shaking, looking at the ceiling, calling out, 'Ambulance.'

I was aware of people running past, people shouting.

Kim was on the phone. I heard her say, 'Thank goodness she is safe,' and I thought, 'That must be her daughter.'

I looked down at my legs and the blood looked even redder, brighter, against the pale blue wash of my jeans. It seemed to be streaming down my legs, covering my new black boots.

'She's losing a lot of blood,' Kim gasped. 'Apply more pressure.'

A paramedic came through and crouched down next to me.

'We need to get her on to a stretcher,' he said.

'My dad,' I kept trying to shout out.

'I know, we'll find him,' Kim said. There were tears streaming down her face as Phil, who I assumed was her husband, tried to remain calm.

A couple more people came towards me. I looked forwards and saw this girl lying in front of me, shaking,

crying, blood down her ankle. She was looking at me, complete horror on her face.

I must look like something from a scary movie, I thought, and I knew then that something was seriously wrong. There was a merchandise stand next to me, so they shoved everything off the surface, folded the legs back up, and put it next to me.

'We need to get you on to the table,' a voice said.

'I'm in too much pain,' I tried to say.

'We have to do it.'

I couldn't really argue as I couldn't speak, so they all gently lifted me and put me on to the table. As soon as they moved me, my left arm fell backwards, as if it were dangling off me, and I screamed the most I'd ever done because the pain was unbearable. The hard, cold surface of the table highlighted all my injuries, my crunching bones, and I felt in even more pain.

'We'll count to three and lift the table,' I heard, and as the table lifted into the air, I remember feeling like I was going to slide straight off, especially as there was blood everywhere making it slippery. I couldn't feel my hands, I couldn't hold on to anything. I tried to concentrate instead on looking straight up at the glass ceiling of the train station. They took me down a flight of steps, which was the worst bit because with each step, the table shuddered, causing my body to vibrate with pain. There were six people taking me down, with Kim and Phil at the back. When we reached the

bottom, they laid me down and ran off to get someone. I could almost hear properly again by this point, and I realised it was really, really loud with lots of people around me.

'Did you come here with your dad?' Kim asked.

'Yes.'

'Do you remember his phone number?'

'I only know the home number.'

I somehow managed to get out the numbers, and Phil went off to use the phone. I assumed he'd end up talking to my mum.

As I lay there, a man came over.

'Hi, Freya, I'm Martyn,' he said.

I remember thinking, *Why are you so cheerful and telling me your name?*

Then, a policewoman arrived.

'Are you Freya?' she asked.

'Yes,' I nodded.

'I'm Clare.'

'Did you enjoy the concert? Wasn't she on that TV show? I heard all her hair had fallen out because she had to dye it red.'

I said 'Yes', but again was confused. *Why is she asking me all these questions?*

When she asked me about the concert it felt like that had never happened. It felt like time had stood still and I had been trapped in this moment for ever, a moment of pain and shock and horror – and torture because

of the monotonous noise of the alarm that was still going off in the building running rings inside my head.

A woman next to me was checking over my arm, the slightest touch making me scream out in pain. A man at my feet said, 'we're going to cut open your jeans properly to look at your legs.' I remember feeling embarrassed and thinking, *I don't want to lie here naked in front of all these strangers.*

As the cold night air hit my skin, I felt ten times more freezing. I started to shake, and they put some kind of blanket over me. I could feel something dripping down my face, the liquid ran into my mouth. I tasted it and realised it was blood – there was so much blood.

My nose and mouth throbbed with pain, it felt like everything was missing, like it wasn't there. I tried not to move my mouth a lot or my tongue around; there was bits of gum hanging out of my mouth, all fleshy and raw – it felt like my whole face was gone.

As they looked at my legs, I heard Phil talking to someone about me, and they said, 'Thank you so much'.

I recognised the voice. It was my dad. I couldn't move my head, but he came running and when I saw him, I wept even more if that was possible. He was crying too and took my hand.

'It's all right, it's all right,' he said, 'I'm here, I'm here.'

'I love you.'

'I love you too.'

'Am I going to die?'

'No, you're going to be fine.'

He kept repeating it but I didn't believe him because I could tell by his face that he was horrified by what he saw. I had never seen him look like that before, all the colour was drained out of his face, he was just white and shaking, his eyes were wide and red.

In that moment, I really thought I was going to die.

My eyes kept wanting to close, and voices kept saying, 'Stay with us, stay with us.'

Because I thought I was dying, I thought about the place that I was the happiest: family holidays to Disneyland in Florida, with my mum and my sister and my dad.

'I love Georgia and Mum,' I said to Dad quietly.

He just nodded at me, because I think it made him too upset.

Time passed. I kept saying on a loop, 'I need an ambulance . . . Where's Nell? . . . What happened to Ariana? . . . I need an ambulance . . . '

Then I heard shouting: 'We need to get to a hospital now.'

They lifted me up and I screamed, the pain just getting worse. I kept wanting to faint as I was losing so much blood.

We went outside. It had now been almost two hours since the explosion, but it felt even longer than that. I was absolutely freezing, I had nothing on my legs

and pretty much nothing on my top so I was basically lying there half-naked. I vaguely felt something being injected into my legs, but my legs were so numb I couldn't actually feel anything.

I was still on the table and this guy put a figure one on it – they had different numbers for different people who needed an ambulance – and then they said, 'Right, it's here'.

They said that they were going to move me onto the stretcher and I became hysterical at the thought of the pain.

'No,' I said.

'You've got no choice,' Dad told me.

'No!' I kept shouting.

Terrified, I screamed, and Dad's face filled with shock at the sheer ferocity of my protests. They put me on the stretcher anyway, loaded me into the ambulance, Dad next to me, holding my hand.

They asked him to sit down.

'Are you serious?!' he replied, swearing.

They saw the look on his face and simply said, 'OK'.

As we started the journey, Dad looked at me.

'Where's Nell?' he asked, softly.

'I don't know,' I replied, my voice small. 'She had been with me . . . I thought she was behind me . . . '

I paused for a moment.

'What happened, Dad?'

'I don't know,' he said, squeezing my hand tightly. 'There was some sort of explosion.'

'Is Ariana OK?'

At this, Dad seem to bristle.

'I don't know!' His voice laced with irritation.

By now, my pain was becoming even more acute, if that was possible.

Seeing me grimacing in agony, Dad appealed to the paramedic to help me.

He turned to me and said, 'Freya, we're going to give you some morphine.'

I was terrified of needles, but I knew I needed it, so they put the injection into my arm and I was overcome with sudden drowsiness.

'I want to close my eyes,' I said to Dad.

'No, you can't,' he kept saying.

I struggled to stay awake, looking at the ceiling. We were driving fast, I was strapped into the stretcher so it didn't hurt. I was even more sure I was going to die, so I tried to think about happy things again. A month before, Harry Styles' song 'Sign Of The Times' had come out, and it made me feel so happy when I listened to it, so I started to try and mouth the words.

'What are you doing?' Dad said.

At that point, I wasn't sure whether I'd ever be able to tell him.

'I need to close my eyes,' I said to Dad, my voice becoming smaller.

Dad looked at the paramedics in anguish.

'That's fine,' he replied, softly.

I closed my eyes, everything fading to black. I don't remember if I actually went to sleep or not, but if I did, it was only for the briefest of moments, as the next thing I knew, we had arrived at the hospital.

CHAPTER FIFTEEN

Brave

As the psychologists packed up their things after our session had finished, I looked at the ceiling, feeling drained, exhausted, but relieved. I said goodbye, then around fifteen minutes later, my parents walked in, looking at me tentatively.

'How did it go?' Mum asked.

'I told them everything,' I replied. 'It all just came out, the concert, the attack. I feel a lot better.'

'Well, you seem a lot more calm then they did,' Dad said. 'We were just chatting to them in the corridor and their faces were white. They said they needed to go and have a coffee!'

Mum looked at the crumpled pieces of tissue in the bin, my eyes red and watery.

'It must have been hard to talk about,' she said.

'I was fine telling them about the concert,' I replied, 'but when it came to the explosion, I was really, really

upset. I was replaying it over in my head. I remembered that when I was with Nell, I had said I loved her, and she said she loved me, and I became overwhelmed. They were giving me tissues and being really nice.'

Mum gave my hand a squeeze.

'They said that you're coping really well,' she said, relief in her eyes. 'We don't know where you get the strength from. Dad and I would lose the plot. You're so brave.'

That word again. Brave. But like I've said before, I just didn't feel brave. It wasn't the right word at all. 'Brave' was for Phil and Kim, who didn't know if their own daughter was alive but looked after me anyway; for the paramedics who ran into the face of danger to help everyone no matter if they got hurt too; for Mum, Dad and Georgia, who came to see me every day and never showed how much it was hurting them.

Over the course of my time in hospital, I'd talked on and off about the night of the 22nd, but I'd never heard my parents' version of events. As they settled into the high-backed chairs where the therapists had sat just beforehand, their version of events naturally unfolded. It was the first time I'd heard about what they had been through, and listening to the pain, fear and horror they'd experienced made me even more determined to be strong and get back on my feet.

CHAPTER SIXTEEN
Dad's Story

After I watched the girls bouncing up the arena steps in their fancy shoes and clothes, I found myself a bench in the railway station, near the stairway up to MEN Arena, and sat doing some work on my laptop while I waited for the concert to finish. Around 10.15 p.m., I noticed the first few concert-goers starting to leave, so I decided to pack up my things and wait for the girls on the walkway that leads to the stairs down into the railway station. I checked my phone for texts from Freya, and at around 10.28 p.m. realised that the booming rhythm of the music had stopped. At the same time the doors from the foyer opened as the audience started to leave the arena.

Based upon the little information I've read since the bombing, I assume that the person responsible for the explosion must have walked past me, but I've seen photographs of him from the night and have no recollection of seeing him.

Then, at what we now know was 10.31 p.m., there was a bang and flash from the foyer, and the lights went out briefly. In the moments that followed, what seemed like a thousand people ran towards me, getting out of the foyer.

Initially I just stood, unable to comprehend what had happened. It didn't occur to me to run with the crowd, I just started walking, initially slowly and then quickly, towards the doors back into the foyer. I remember that there was some smoke coming out of the partly open doors, and also that the crowd running out of the foyer had ended.

I opened the doors, and entered the foyer. The images of what I then saw are very vivid, and horrific beyond words. The light was dim, and there was smoke in the air. The floor was littered with bodies, some moving, others not. There were also some walking wounded. I had no real idea what had happened, but my mind was drawn straight away to the fact that there must have been a bomb.

I believe that it was at this point that I first called Alison at home, to tell her that something terrible had happened. I was shaking when I called her. I told her that there had been an explosion and that I thought it had been a bomb. I said that I needed to look for Freya and also that I needed to try calling her mobile. I then began to move around the foyer, looking for Freya. I walked among the bodies, searching. During my search, I came to a spot where it was clear that the bomb had been detonated: there was debris everywhere, the ground was blackened and had been ripped up. I saw a hand on that spot and a number

of internal organs, including what I recognised to be intestines. Presumably these belonged to the suicide bomber.

Having failed to find Freya in the foyer, I then went into the arena concourse, and started calling Freya's mobile repeatedly. Sometimes it rang before going to answerphone, other times it went straight to answerphone. This led me to believe that she must be trying to call me. I rushed out of the concourse and down the steps leading from the main Arena entrance.

I then called Alison again, who was crying. She said that she had also been trying Freya's mobile, and had also sent her a text. I said that I was confused about what had happened but would carry on looking. I then hung up and went to send Freya a text myself, at which point I noted that I had an unread message. It was from Freya, timed at 10.31 p.m., and read 'On our way!! Xx'. I now know that this text was sent at almost precisely the same moment as the bomb was detonated.

I texted back 'Please please ring me!!!!' at 10.41 p.m.

The emergency services had started to arrive in force by this time. I kept trying to call Freya and called Alison a number of times and we both said that we were certain that Freya was dead. One of Alison's friends, Amanda, texted me to say that she had seen that there had been an incident on the news and was checking everything was OK. I called her and asked her to go straight to our house to support Alison. I sent Freya another text at 11.19 p.m. At some stage I ran up the car-park ramp and back to my car, where I put my laptop bag back in the boot.

When I got back to the road outside the Arena, the police had by this time cordoned it off, preventing me from going back towards the railway station. I stood in the road, and then found a police officer. I told them that Freya and Nell were missing and explained that Freya was not answering her phone. At this stage, I was now really convinced that our daughter was dead, although some part of me could not accept this.

At 11.35 p.m., I had a text from Amanda to say that Nell's mum had arrived at our house. As I was reading this, I had a text from Alison that read 'Man found her, ring' and then a mobile number. I can't describe that feeling but it was the biggest adrenaline surge I've ever experienced. The phone was answered by a man who I later learned was Phil Dick. Phil explained that he and his wife were with my daughter, inside the railway station. I think that he said that she was badly injured but was alive and safe, but I am not certain.

My overwhelming reaction was to run to her, but this was not possible because they were some 500 metres away from me, well within the police cordon. I ran to a police officer near the main arena steps and explained that my daughter was alive and within the railway station. I still had Phil Dick on the line and I gave my telephone to the officer and he spoke to a colleague near Freya, who Phil had handed his phone to. Between them, the officers verified that my explanation was true and I was allowed within the cordon and escorted up the road and into the railway station entrance.

I was greeted by a scene of carnage, with the emergency services treating the injured in every available bit of floor space. I was quickly shown to Freya, who was lying on a makeshift stretcher near to the railway station exit. She was very distressed and I was severely shocked by her physical appearance. My instinct was to hold her, but it was clear that her injuries made this impossible, so all I could do was to talk to her and try to comfort her. The initial euphoria at her being alive was rapidly overtaken by concern about her injuries. In my mind, I could not believe that they were not life-threatening, and I was certain that they would be life-changing.

In total, Freya was missing and in our minds probably dead for almost exactly one hour. The depth of pain that we felt during this hour, which was the longest of our lives, is indescribable. If I then reflect upon the situation for the families of those who were lost in this tragedy, including Nell, many of whom were uncertain of the fate of their loved ones for up to forty-eight hours in some cases, I simply become numb. There can be no words to describe what they have gone through and must continue to deal with for the rest of their lives.

CHAPTER SEVENTEEN
Mum's Story

I was sitting in the conservatory watching TV with the door shut, not wanting the noise to wake Georgia who had an exam the next day, when around 10.40 p.m. the phone rang. It was Nick. He sounded strange, a hesitation in his voice.

He said there had been an explosion, he thought it was a bomb. He was looking for Freya and Nell and asked if I had heard from them. I instantly felt sick, a mixture of horror and sheer panic. When I said I hadn't heard from Freya, he said he had to go and keep looking for them and he would ring me back.

I sat alone in total shock as the news sank in. My heart was pounding and I started to shake uncontrollably. I kept repeating 'Freya, where are you?' out loud and in my head over and over again. I grabbed my mobile and tried ringing her number but there was no answer. I also sent texts telling her to ring me and that I loved her. Nick rang back

about ten minutes later but it seemed like an eternity. I was shaking so much that I struggled to speak.

'Have you found her?' I asked. 'No.' 'Have you heard from her?' 'No.' At this point I became more tearful and distressed, shouting 'Where is she?' and really starting to believe that she was dead. This time, I could hear lots of noise and sirens in the background, which only added to my stress and panic. Nick ended the call quickly in case Freya tried to contact him and to continue his search.

I went to the computer and started searching the web for any news on the MEN Arena but found nothing on either national or local news sites. This gave me some hope that it wasn't as serious as we thought. The phone rang again, and I hoped with all of my heart that it was Freya, but it was Nick with no positive news. He was starting to sound desperate and frantic. He told me to try and find a phone number for Nell's mum and dad and tell them the situation. I looked through some old phone books we had under the stairs and searched online but couldn't find anything. This made me feel even more distressed and I was becoming almost hysterical, but I was conscious that I didn't want to wake up Georgia so did my best to keep my sobs under control. I also felt freezing and was shaking violently. I wrapped up in a blanket and rocked back and forth, sat in the conservatory.

At this stage I was in total shock. I was overwhelmed with disbelief that this was happening to me but was convinced that my beautiful little girl was gone and that I would never

see her again. I had lost both of my parents in the last couple of years, my mum only four months previously, but the pain I felt at that moment was piercing, unbearable, and will stay with me for the rest of my life. My parents lost my brother several years ago and I always knew that to lose a child is every parent's worst nightmare, and now I felt I understood.

The phone rang again. Nick had still not found them. He told me my friend Amanda was on her way to sit with me and kept repeating that I needed to get hold of Nell's parents. The conversation ended abruptly; he had to keep searching.

I felt useless, I wanted to join the search but was stranded far away, sat by the phone and praying that Freya would ring. Minutes seemed like an eternity. How was I going to tell Georgia that something had happened to her sister? The thought of telling her was so unbearable that I just left her asleep. The home phone rang and it was a male voice and he asked if I was Freya's mum. He said that he was with Freya and that she was OK. He told me that she had injuries but they were not life-changing. The man was very calm and sounded very kind and through my sobs I thanked him from the bottom of my heart. I told him that Nick was there and searching for her. He told me to put the phone down, ring the number back, copy it down and then give it to Nick. He would then tell him where to find them.

I was shaking so much that it took me three attempts to write the number down. I then rang Nick to tell him

that Freya had been found. We were both in pieces but still concerned that there was no news about Nell. I gave the number for Nick to ring but he called straight back to say it was the wrong number. Again shaking, I rang the number again and realised that I had copied a digit wrong. I rang Nick again with the correct number and he hurried off the phone to try and locate Freya.

Amanda turned up at the door and we hugged and the tears flowed. We sat huddled together, awaiting further news from Nick, and it felt like for ever. There was a knock at the door and a lady I had not met before who looked very anxious asked if I knew what was happening; it was Nell's mum, Jayne. She had heard something on the news but did not know the extent of what had happened at the Arena. I explained that I had been trying to contact her but could not find her number; she told me that they were ex-directory.

The three of us sat together waiting for further news. None of us really spoke, other than the odd word; Jayne and I were both shaking and very anxious. Nick rang to say that he had been reunited with Freya and that she was OK; at this point he only told me that she had a broken arm. The relief that I felt was overwhelming but I found the thought that she must be in a lot of pain and that I wasn't by her side very hard to cope with. I asked Nick if they had found Nell or if she was with Freya but he said not. Relaying this news to her mum was very difficult. Amanda and I tried to comfort Jayne as she kept repeating that she had a bad feeling about Nell.

She rang her husband, Ernie, and decided to go home and sit with him to await further news. I promised to contact them as soon as I had any more information. I was worried about her driving home alone in such a state. How could a night that started off with so much excitement have turned to such horror? Nick rang again and told me I needed to get to Manchester as quickly as possible. Obviously still in shock, I told him that Georgia was asleep and I couldn't wake her up as she had an exam in the morning. He repeated that I needed to get to Manchester now. He told me to wake her up and head towards the city; he said that he would tell me which hospital Freya was being admitted to as we got nearer. At this stage I started to think that Freya must have serious injuries but Nick just kept repeating that she had a broken arm. Knowing she had been injured by a bomb conjured up horrific injuries in my mind, mostly relating to loss of limbs. I could hear lots of noise in the background during the phone calls and could often hear Freya shouting out, obviously in pain. I was distraught.

I went upstairs to wake Georgia, who came round quickly; she had heard the phone ringing and also the front door, but had assumed that the latter was Freya coming home. I told her that there had been an accident, an explosion, that her sister was OK but injured, and that we needed to get to the hospital. Although clearly shocked, she remained calm and got dressed quickly. I grabbed Molly, Freya's special bear, and squeezed her tight. Amanda insisted on driving us to Manchester as I was in no fit state.

The car journey was long and arduous. The roads were incredibly quiet. Amanda hates using motorways, so we took the back roads to Manchester. She drove as fast as she could, disregarding speed limits and only stopping at traffic lights when she really had to. We were all very quiet with our own thoughts, muttering occasional words of comfort to each other. I reached over to Georgia in the back of the car intermittently to check she was OK and squeeze her hand. I sat hugging Molly tightly, willing Freya to hold on and counting the seconds until I was back with her; I just wanted to see her. On the way, Nick rang to say that they were heading for the Royal Manchester Children's Hospital and to meet them there.

On arrival at RMCH, Georgia and I ran to the Accident & Emergency department whilst Amanda parked the car. At reception, we gave Freya's name but were told that she would arrive in ten minutes so we were to take a seat in the waiting area. The waiting room was eerily quiet with only a couple of other people. There was a girl there with a bandaged leg hobbling around and I wondered if she had been at the Ariana concert. A nurse then announced that only one parent was allowed in the waiting area and other family and friends would have to wait in another room. Georgia reluctantly went off with Amanda whilst I sat alone, desperate to see and hold Freya.

Suddenly Nick appeared at the doorway; for some reason I had not noticed the ambulance arrive. Freya was in the resus area but Nick did not want me to see her yet. At this

point he told me the full extent of what he knew of her injuries, but I insisted that I wanted to see her immediately. Nick and I did not cry or hug each other; we were both solely focused on Freya and keeping as calm as possible.

I walked into the resus room, where I could see Freya on a stretcher, surrounded by doctors and nurses. They parted to let me squeeze her hand. She had an oxygen mask on but I noticed that her face was covered in blood. I told her that I was here now and that she would be OK.

We stepped away from Freya whilst the staff carried on with their assessments. There were so many people around her that there simply was not enough room around the bed for us too. At this point we could no longer see her, which in some ways was distressing, but everyone around her was so focused upon examining her that we just knew that it was the right thing to do. Freya had been given quite a bit of morphine at this point and really wanted to go to sleep. She kept trying to speak to us and we couldn't understand her, which caused her to get very frustrated and agitated. Eventually, we realised that she was saying that she couldn't go to sleep because she still had her contact lenses in! We told her to take them out. She removed the one from the right eye (without the aid of a mirror because she did not want to see herself) but couldn't get the one out of her left. There then ensued a panic, with nurses and doctors shining lights into her left eye. After a few minutes, it was established that she didn't have her left contact lens in, and it was concluded that it must have

come out during the bomb blast. Freya, however, refused to get her head around this and continued to worry about it.

I decided to go and look for Georgia; she and Amanda had been taken to another waiting area. I found a police officer who had been looking after them. He asked me a few questions and took some notes before checking with one of the nursing staff that it was OK to go and get them. He returned shortly after with both of them and we exchanged brief hugs. I asked Georgia if she wanted to see Freya and she nodded, so I took her through to the A&E bay. Freya seemed to recognise her and Georgia touched her hand and said 'Hiya, Baba!' She was really struggling with seeing Freya, who was covered in blood and looked in incredible pain, so Amanda took her back into the waiting area.

The main trauma consultant who was in charge at this point was an older, very tall guy. He was nice, but extremely businesslike and thorough, and didn't tell us very much about what was going on. We didn't really ask any questions either, as we just felt that we needed to let them get on with their work. At around 1.45 a.m. we were told that Freya needed X-rays and scans, and so we walked next to her trolley down to the X-ray department, which was nearby. We recall being amazed at the size of the entourage that came with us.

The X-ray room was really big, but it was filled with people. There were so many that there was barely enough room for them to all fit behind the protection screens as

the X-rays were being taken. We were given lead-lined gowns so that we could stay with Freya as the X-rays were being taken. Trying to get Freya in the correct position for the X-rays was very difficult and was incredibly painful for her. She screamed at many points, but we don't think that she cried.

I still clutched Molly continuously; I had offered her to Freya on a few occasions but she was worried that she would get blood on her so wouldn't take her. It was during our time in X-ray that I first really saw Freya's face close up and I found the sight of her cuts very distressing. It was also when I became acutely aware of the smell of explosives in Freya's hair, and this continued to haunt me for many days to come, every time I went to kiss her.

At this stage, Freya was still wearing what remained of her clothing. We were told that we would have to change her into a hospital gown, but clearly this was impossible. The solution was to cut the clothes off her and then drape a gown and blanket over her. This process was very upsetting for a number of reasons. We were able to observe her injuries and see just what a terrible state she was in; it was like a scene from the worst horror movie you could imagine. When they cut her clothes, they were removed very carefully and placed in plastic bags which were then labelled. We were told that they were being sent to Forensics and would be used as evidence. This brought the reality of the situation into focus and made us both feel physically sick. At around 4.30 a.m. a team

of anaesthetists arrived and escorted us to theatre. Freya was conscious and we spoke to her and did our best to comfort her as we made the journey. We tried to keep beside her but kept having to fall back at doorways and corners; hopefully we did not get in the way. We tried to go with her but the room was packed with people and we couldn't stay whilst she went under. We gave her a kiss and told her we loved her; she didn't look scared at all, but we were petrified. 'Please take care of her,' I told them as we left. The surgeons warned us that it would be a very long surgery, but didn't quantify what that actually meant in terms of hours. Nick, Georgia and I all hugged for the first time when we were stood together outside the theatre doors and the tears flowed.

Even though it was the worst night of my life, the medical team had been amazing, and I was so grateful that I still had Freya in front of me.

CHAPTER EIGHTEEN
Operation Wheelchair

Hearing Mum and Dad's accounts of what happened on the night of the attack was incredibly emotional and difficult, giving me a newfound appreciation for just how strong they were. They'd been plunged into every parent's worst nightmare, and there were moments which were particularly distressing – I winced when Dad described how he'd come across the bomber's body parts as he'd frantically searched for me in the foyer.

Mum got angry at Dad as he described the moment, snapping, 'She doesn't need to know that.' But I did need to know. It crystallised in my mind how lucky I was to have survived.

'How have you coped with what you saw?' I asked Dad, amazed at how he still managed to retain his sense of humour and be strong for us all, having witnessed such horror.

He confided that when I was first admitted to hospital, he had been suffering from terrifying flashbacks, but while I was in the ICU the psychologists had given him some invaluable advice. They gave him the idea of writing down his memories from the night. They explained that the idea behind doing this is that it allows the mind to put everything in some sort of order, so that the memories can then be filed away, available when you want them but not jumping into your thoughts when you don't.

'I have to be honest and say that I was sceptical about this principle,' Dad said, 'but over the coming evenings, when all was quiet, I tried it out. I compiled my recollection of the night and the effect on my flashbacks was incredible. They stopped within a few days.' I listened to him, thinking once again that I never wanted to cause them suffering ever again.

I must try to stay positive.

The next day, I set my sights on a new goal.

'I want to try and go in the wheelchair today,' I announced to Mum.

'Really?' she replied, surprised.

It was a big step, as it would require me sitting up, shuffling to the side of the bed, standing on my own momentarily without the aid of the wheelie trolley, and then finally sitting down in the chair: a four-step plan. But I was determined to do it.

So, when my physio, Vicky, came in for the first of my twice-daily sessions, I told her about Operation Wheelchair.

'Great idea!' she replied enthusiastically. 'Let's do this!'

And, with that, she rushed off to get a wheelchair before I could change my mind. I think she was pleased to see me being proactive about my recovery, rather than having to be cajoled into doing my exercises like the previous three and a half weeks.

'You're making such good progress,' she said, wheeling a chair to the side of the bed. 'You've gone from needing five of us to get you out of bed to just me!'

I smiled at the realisation. The exercises were vital to my recovery and I was going to put one hundred per cent into them from now on.

Saying that, each step of Operation Wheelchair took so much strength as my body was weighed down by the frame on my left arm and the boots on my legs. But I thought about Mum and Dad, that horrifying hour when they were frantically trying to find me, losing hope that I was alive, and was determined to do it for them.

I managed to sit up on the side of the bed, then, with the help of Vicky, I tentatively put one foot down, and then the other, using the bed frame for support. I wobbled on my jelly-legs, threatening to give way at any moment, but I fixed my gaze on the wheelchair to balance myself.

'You're standing!' Mum clapped, her face filled with joy as she quickly whipped out her phone to capture the moment.

Smiling, I felt happy that I'd made her happy.

I looked up, and there, on the other side of the room, was a window. All I could see was the sky. I could tell by the perfect wash of bright blue that it was hot outside, which was a strange thought as it was dim on the ward in comparison and I was constantly swaddled in sheets. As I gazed at this perfect summer's day, my heart sang – it was the first time I'd seen the outside world and it made me feel like I was one tiny step closer to going home. I took a picture of this moment in my head and made a promise to myself to never take the world for granted again.

We managed to get me into the wheelchair – tricky as I was still attached to a lot of tubes, in my arms, up my nose, and my catheter. As I wiggled around, adjusting myself in the seat, Vicky looked so proud.

'Well done!' she said. 'Now off you go! Enjoy!'

'Come on then,' Mum said, her voice firm, and she began pushing me out of my isolated room in the Burns Unit, down the corridor, through the double doors and into the main hospital area. I was instantly bathed in daylight as the sun streamed in through the large windows on either side of us, and I blinked, taken aback, my eyes taking a moment to adjust.

'Whoah,' I said, as I greedily drank in my surroundings. I couldn't believe how modern the hospital was, it looked more like a shopping centre with its high ceilings and sleek, contemporary architecture. 'This place is amazing,' I said to Mum.

'It's not bad, is it?' Mum laughed.

As she pushed me along, she pointed out the spot outside the High Dependency Unit near the large window where everyone went to make phone calls due to its half-decent reception.

'Dad used to sit on that ledge there, updating everyone on your progress,' Mum said, pointing to the windowsill.

Then she wheeled me past the Intensive Care Unit.

'That's where they took you when you first came in.'

Mum paused at a pair of double doors, so innocuous that it seemed unbelievable to think that just three weeks before, the ward had been a scene of organised chaos as the hospital faced one of its biggest challenges to date, treating seriously injured victims of the attack and providing a sanctuary for their devastated families.

'It's so colourful,' I gasped as I took in all the rainbow-coloured walls and beautifully painted murals bursting with underwater scenes, astronauts, space-ships, animals and cute characters.

It really brought home to me how many children must be here. I'd been in relative isolation since arriving in hospital, and hadn't spoken to any other patients, though I knew that Mum and Dad had bonded with some other families of children who'd been injured in the attack.

'So, these are the lifts we take to go outside,' said Mum, stopping by a pair of shiny silver doors. 'We

can go down in them if you like. I can show you the Costa coffee and café we go to?'

I looked at them, worried.

'Are there mirrors in there?' I asked.

'Yes.'

'Can you please take me in backwards? I don't want to see myself.'

'OK,' Mum replied, no questions asked.

She wheeled me around, and pressed the button. A few minutes later, the doors pinged open and Mum manoeuvred me inside.

'There's a Marks & Spencer there too,' Mum said, lightening the mood as we travelled down. 'Here we are.'

The doors opened, and within seconds it was as if we'd entered another world. Upstairs, it had been relatively quiet as Mum pushed me around, but here, in the main hub of the hospital, we were in the thick of things as people rushed in and out of the shops and cafés, doctors strode along purposefully, toddlers clutched their parents' hands, and poorly looking children with tubes running up their noses were pushed along in wheelchairs. As I took it all in, it didn't register in my head that I was one of them too.

'So, this is where we get sandwiches sometimes,' Mum said, taking me towards the café.

I peered inside, and saw that there was a long queue of people lining up at a Subway sandwich kiosk. The

smell of toasting bread was making me feel hungry, a feeling I hadn't experienced in a long time. It felt good.

'And down that way is the exit, and opposite is Ronald McDonald House,' Mum said, continuing her tour.

There were large windows on either side of the door leading outside, and as I looked through the glass, I got my first glimpse of the invaluable 'home from home' where Mum, Dad and Georgia, along with other families who had children in hospital, were able to get some rest and cook dinner. From the outside, it looked a bit like a fancy Travel Lodge with an inviting-looking patch of grass outside.

'We'll have a picnic there one day soon,' I said to Mum.

'Good idea,' she replied, smiling. 'They have a beautiful garden out the back. We can go there too.'

It felt strange to see this new world in which Mum, Dad and Georgia had been living in without me for the last three and a half weeks, but it also brought me comfort to see that they weren't alone. It was also a big milestone to be in the wheelchair, experiencing life outside of the four walls of my cubicle.

But my creeping exhaustion was also a reminder that I had a way to go yet. My neck was hurting from keeping upright in the wheelchair for so long and I was starting to hanker for my bed.

'Dad and Georgia are on their way,' Mum said, wheeling me to a bank of comfy seats so she could have a sit down herself. 'We'll wait for them here.'

A couple of minutes later, they arrived, all smiles at seeing me out and about.

'I'll push you back,' Dad said, grasping the chance to steer me around the hospital.

We made our way back to the lifts, with Dad and Georgia pointing out sights along the way as if they were tour guides.

'They do the best lattes in there,' Georgia said, nodding at the Costa. I thought back to all the times that I'd stopped off for a coffee with my friends while out shopping on a Saturday afternoon. Before the attack, I'd really gotten into chai lattes, making me feel all sophisticated and grown-up, sat in one of those big brown leather armchairs, sipping from a fancy tall glass mug. Now, I couldn't drink anything other than water from a straw from my child-like Disney Princess cup, and even that would go everywhere. Mum would try and feed the straw into my mouth and it would spill all over, making me feel like I was drowning.

Sorry! Mum would say, dabbing it off with a tissue.

I wistfully thought back to those coffee breaks. At some point in the future, even if I didn't know when that would be yet, I was determined that I would go shopping with my friends again and taste another chai latte, and this time I would cherish the moment.

We arrived at the lifts and were chatting amongst ourselves when the doors slid open. I looked up and

suddenly gasped. Staring back at me was the reflection of someone I didn't recognise at all.

Me. My whole face was covered in black specks. There was a giant cut all around my mouth, dominating my entire face, and another cut below my eye. The wounds looked red, raw and painful, like the fleshy inside of a peach, and my face was ghostly pale and swollen.

The bottom edge of the mirror stopped at the top half of my shoulders, but I could just about make out the big metal pole stuck in my left arm, and even though I knew that I had the frame piecing my limb back together, it was a shock to see the state that I was really in, a mangle of wounds and metal.

I started crying. I couldn't help it. The image I was confronted with was so far removed from the image I'd had in my head of what I thought I looked like.

That person still looked like me, the Freya with the big blue eyes, long blonde hair and wide, toothy smile, but with just a few cuts.

This Freya looked like she was wearing a Halloween mask, only the horrifying reality was that I couldn't take it off.

'I'm sorry, I'm sorry,' Dad said, quickly turning me around, but it was too late. I'd already seen myself. I think we were all shocked by what had happened and returned to the Burns Unit in numb silence. The image replayed over and over in my head until I went to sleep.

CHAPTER NINETEEN
Ups and Downs

Physio had become non-negotiable, and now I could use a wheelchair it was time for a whole new challenge. With no 'ifs' or 'buts', my physiotherapists got me into the chair, then wheeled me back down to the main hub of the hospital with the cafés and shops, and through some heavy double doors.

My stomach sank. We were in a proper gym, large and airy, with yoga balls and weights. Don't get me wrong – the room was nice and whoever was in charge of the gym had tried to make it even friendlier with lots of colourful artwork on the wall. But I absolutely hated doing PE at school, and seeing all this exercise equipment instantly took me back to gym class and made me feel like a fish out of water. I took a deep breath. There was work to do.

There were two long metal railings running along the middle of the gym, and I was positioned at one

end, with Sarah behind me, Vicky in front and Mum hovering in the background.

'Now try and stand up,' Vicky said, face full of encouragement.

By this point, I knew my physios had hearts of gold and they were doing everything they could to get me better, so I looked at the railings and thought, *OK, I will do it for them*. As I tried to stand up, I was shaking so much I was basically a plate of jelly. I was so weak and so thin – just 39 kilos – and didn't feel in control of my own body. It sounds weird, but I was out of practice at moving myself. I was also suffering from an internal monologue: *I have broken bones in my legs so how can I walk on them? It will be all wobbly and crunchy, and surely I'll topple over and smash my left arm even more as I am the clumsiest person in the world.*

But you can't make an omelette without breaking eggs. It took a minute for me to stand properly on my feet, as my left arm, straightened by the frame, was completely out of action, which meant I only had my right hand to balance with, and that was still very weak. I put my hand on the railing – it felt so weird to grip something as I had barely moved my arms in weeks.

I shakily stood up, my arm wobbling.

'Try and take a step,' Vicky urged.

My legs, weighed down by my bulky, removable lower-leg casts (air boots, as the doctors called them)

– a hefty 3 kilograms each – felt so heavy and cumbersome, as if I were an astronaut being pulled down by gravity.

I took two small steps and quickly sat back down, scared that I was going to topple forward.

There's no way I can do this, I thought, trembling.

But then I looked at Mum and she was crying.

'Come on, Freya,' she said, tears running down her face. 'You can do it!'

I looked up, and saw that it wasn't just Mum rooting for me. A crowd of hospital staff had gathered, including my dental team, who were waiting to talk to me and were cheering me on. I felt an added pressure because of the audience, but seeing the number of people who were helping me all in one place – and this wasn't even all of them – really spurred me on.

Then I noticed one very special visitor standing in the doorway: Alfie the Pug. He was the hospital therapy dog and was a bundle of cuteness in his bright-green RMCH T-shirt.

'We'll let him come in and you can stroke him if you take a few steps,' Sarah said with a cheeky smile as she caught me looking at Alfie adoringly. Seeing him made me miss my own chocolate-brown spaniel, Milo. Since the night of the attack, he'd been looked after by our neighbours, and I was desperate to give him a cuddle.

'OK, I'm going to walk for Alfie the Pug.' I laughed. I struggled onto my feet again, gripped the railing

with my one semi-good hand and, slowly, shuffled forward.

I could hear cheering as I carried on moving forward, which motivated me even more. All these people wanted me to get better and I had to do it.

As I tentatively put one foot in front of the other, I also started thinking about all the people back home in Holmes Chapel who were thinking about me, everyone on the blog who had left messages wishing me well, and then Nell. Just before the concert, Nell had hurt her ankle and had been on crutches, and I remember playfully teasing her whilst she hobbled around. So, in the back of my head, I thought, *Come on, Nell would be laughing at you so much right now for not taking a step.*

I had to do it for her.

After I reached around ten small steps, I took a break, then set myself a goal of another ten.

Then, slowly, slowly, in blocks of a dozen steps, I managed to walk eight metres – a small distance but it felt like miles. The room erupted into applause and I remember feeling tears in my eyes because I felt so happy – not only because I'd managed to do it for everyone who had rallied around me, but because it made me feel like everyone else, and I was so desperate to feel like I was just one in a crowd again.

Sarah and Vicky helped me back into my wheelchair and the moment I sank into the seat, I slumped in exhaustion.

'Well done!' Mum said, beaming at me at with me with one of the biggest smiles I'd seen since being here. 'You were amazing. I'm so proud of you!'

I looked back at her, and I must admit, it did suddenly feel like a miracle: a miracle that I'd somehow survived the attack, and that now I'd just managed to walk for the first time.

Vicky came over, all smiles, carrying Alfie the Pug in her arms, and placed him in my lap. I beamed at his cartoon-character face, with his little pink tongue sticking out of the corner of his crinkled mouth and big brown eyes like pools of melted dark chocolate gazing at me. I stroked his shiny golden coat, and thought, *Today is a good day*. I felt like I'd really achieved something for everyone.

CHAPTER TWENTY

Food

As we knew they at one point would, the police came by to take my statement about what happened on 22nd May. Mum, Dad, Georgia and I sat together for around an hour as the police took down my recollections from the night. I tried my best to stay calm throughout, but when it came to talking about Nell, I broke down. It was a stark reminder that, yes, I was injured, and yes, I would have scars – but I had survived. I don't know why I survived, or how I had survived, but I had.

That commitment to getting better for my family, and then for everyone else who'd supported me, was morphing into something more. I felt like I owed it to everyone who had lost their lives that night to make the most of every moment. To do this, I knew I needed to get my strength up and that meant eating. The feeding tube threaded up my nose was a constant

physical reminder of how ill I was, so to get rid of it, I needed to fuel my body with food.

Shortly after the police left, I looked at Mum.

'Mum, I really fancy eating your spaghetti today.'

'What?' came the reply, as a surprised Mum looked at Dad and Georgia. They'd desperately been trying to get me to eat for nearly four weeks, making lists of possible foods which were soft enough for me to chew, trying to tempt me with fruit, cheese, soup, yoghurt – and now here I was announcing that I'd like to eat Mum's legendary pasta.

'I'm going to make it now!' Mum said, sprinting cheetah-like out of the room and over to Ronald McDonald House, where they had proper kitchens so families could cook their own meals. She returned around an hour later, cradling a Tupperware bowl of steaming spaghetti so carefully that you'd think it was a newborn baby. Auntie Elaine and Kristian had come to visit and were following behind.

'Mmmm, that smells so good,' Kristian said, licking his lips.

The smell of onions and garlic wafted into the cubicle, making me feel instantly hungry.

'Here, Elaine, would you like to do the honours?' Mum said, passing Auntie Elaine the Tupperware, while tucking a napkin underneath my chin.

'OK,' she beamed, carefully twirling spaghetti around the fork.

She gently put it to my lips, and I slurped the pasta into my mouth. As I hadn't eaten anything solid in so long, it felt like I had almost forgotten how to swallow. The sensation was strange at first, but the rich tomato sauce was so delicious, instantly washing away the horrible taste in the back of my throat left behind from the feeding tube. It reminded me of home and all the happy times we'd sat perched on high stools at our breakfast bar, tucking into big bowls of spaghetti, while Milo jumped around our legs, hoping some might be thrown his way. It was amazing how something as simple as a wholesome bowl of pasta could me feel human again. Now I understood the expression 'food for the soul'.

I managed around five mouthfuls before I started to feel really full, but then something in my brain kept saying, 'Keep on eating. You need this to get home.'

Kristian nudged his mum.

'Can I feed it to her?' he asked, looking at me cheekily.

'No!' replied Auntie Elaine, 'You'll get it everywhere!'

'I won't,' he pleaded, 'I'll be extra careful.'

Mum laughed. 'Oh, go on, let him. It's a big moment.'

Auntie Elaine reluctantly handed him the tub, and he guided a huge forkful of spaghetti towards my mouth. On its way, the strands started to unravel perilously and, before we knew it, he'd poured it all down me!

'Oh, Kristian!' Auntie Elaine sighed with an 'I-knew-it' look, as I sat splattered in tomato sauce and wormy

pasta. I found it hysterical and found myself properly laughing until my belly ached for the first time since I'd been in hospital.

The day's events didn't stop there. After Auntie Elaine and Kristian left, and Mum and Georgia had gone over to Ronald McDonald House for a bite to eat, I received a surprise visitor. The moment he walked in, Dad and I started to cry.

I remembered him instantly: It was Martyn, the paramedic who had cared for me as I lay on the train station floor for the two hours or so until the ambulance had arrived.

'Hello, Freya,' he said, his face relaxing with relief to see me sitting up and smiling. 'It's so nice to see you. I've been trying to find you for ages.'

Turns out, he'd only known my first name so had been ringing around all the hospitals trying to track me down.

'We were just talking about you today,' Dad said, 'The police came to take Freya's statement.'

'How was it?' Martyn asked.

'Not easy,' I replied. 'But, it made me realise how many people helped me, people like you, so thank you.'

Dad and I felt so touched that Martyn had been trying so hard to find me. The fact that he took so much time and effort was incredible – another person to whom we owed a debt of gratitude that we could never repay.

CHAPTER TWENTY-ONE

Eyes on the Prize

I woke up feeling groggy. Through bleary eyes, I saw Dad taking down the shrine of cards and photos Georgia had put up for me around my cubicle.

'Morning, sleepyhead,' he smiled. 'We're moving to Ward 78 today.'

'What?' I asked, confused.

I had no idea what – or where – this mythical Ward 78 was, but it came as a bit of a relief to be moving out of the isolated confines of Burns.

I was trundled down through the hospital to my new home. As soon we entered through the double doors it was a sensory overload; I'd gone from the pin-drop quiet of Burns with my own room, to a large open ward full of noise and people. There were rows of beds in bays of four running up the ward, with colourful pictures and decorations everywhere. I was wheeled into my bay, and noticed three of the beds

were already occupied with two children in front of me, and one beside me. I suddenly felt really self-conscious and awkward for the first time, and now that I could sit up more, it meant that my scary injured face was clear for all to see.

I glanced around nervously. *I wonder what they think of me? I'll have to say what happened to me.* It felt the IVs in me were suddenly dribbling panic into my veins instead of drugs. I wished that I could go straight back to my box in Burns – something I'd thought I'd never feel. 'Can you please shut the curtains?' I asked Mum and Dad, shakily. They looked as shell-shocked as I was, and pulled the blue patterned cloth around us, creating a comforting shield. 'I don't want to stay here,' I said. 'How am I going to sleep?'

'You'll be OK,' Mum replied, packing my things away into the bedside drawers.

'Mum's right,' Dad added, 'it might take a while for us get used to it here but, remember, this is your last leg in hospital.'

In that moment, Dad's words really hit me. He was right, being here meant that I was a massive step closer to going home – literally – as Ward 78 was physically closer to the exit of the hospital. There was light at the end of the tunnel. I gave myself my now-familiar internal pep-talk and didn't give the change of scene another thought.

The next day, the OTs came by the ward clutching a giant laminated poster with five pictures of Harry

Styles on it. Across the top, written in big red letters, were the words: 'Freya Lewis's Steps To Home'.

'What's this?' I asked, instantly interested in the dreamy pictures of my favourite singer.

'It's a special chart Charlotte and I made just for you,' Vicky said, proudly showing off their handiwork. 'It's all the steps you need to do before you can go home.'

My eyes eagerly scanned over the poster. There were eight steps:

 i. Car transfer assessment
 ii. Stair assessment
iii. Mobilise around ward
 iv. Mobilise to toilet/bathroom
 v. Assessment with one crutch
 vi. Daily lower-limb exercises using physio tool
vii. Assist with washing and dressing
viii. Daily upper-limb and hand exercises using physio tool

'So, I need to walk on my own with a crutch, walk up some stairs . . . I'm already halfway there with the walking! Surely this won't take me *that* long?'

'You're going to ace it,' Vicky replied, 'But we've got to work hard, get you up and about.'

'Thanks, Vicky,' I said, 'This is so cool. I love it.'

I was so touched by all the effort my physios had ploughed into making me my own personal poster – yet

another example of the love and positivity that was surrounding us.

Now that I could see a tangible end in sight, I was full of motivation to push through the steps. I kept the poster next to my bed so that I'd be able to see it every day.

'There's no time like the present,' Dad piped up. 'Do you want a tour of Ronald McDonald House?'

'OK,' I replied, intrigued. I sat up, inched to the side of the bed, stood up, then managed to shuffle into the wheelchair. Flopping down and peering at my Disney-princess PJ bottoms (are you sensing a theme here?), I looked at Mum.

'Mum, could you do me a favour and cover me up?' I asked. 'I don't want people seeing me in these. I look like I'm seven!'

'I don't think anyone cares, but OK.' She rolled her eyes, smiling, swaddling me up so tightly in blankets that only my face was peeking out. I must have looked like ET.

Dad pushed me out of the ward as Mum and Georgia followed us toward the exit. It was the first time I was going outside in almost a month, and as the artificial lights changed to bright daylight, I winced. It was warm and windy, and a gust of air hit my face – the only patch of skin showing – sending a chill sailing down my body. But it was a-*mazing*. I savoured the moment, like having a bottle of fridge-cold cola on a really hot

day. 'The breeze feels strange but nice,' I beamed. We crossed the road over to the place which had been a lifeline to my family – and many others with children in the hospital – for the last four weeks.

'It's just like a hotel in here,' I said, as Dad showed me their room. It was nicely decorated, with twin beds and an ensuite, reminding me of motels we'd stayed in when we'd gone on road-trips around the States.

'Let's show Freya the kitchen,' Mum said. I don't know what I was expecting, but I was shocked to be wheeled into a large dining hall divided in two – one side had a line of table and chairs like a restaurant set next to a wall of windows with views over Manchester, and the other side had a row of self-contained fully fitted kitchens with fridges and cupboards so each family had their own cooking station.

'It's like being on *Masterchef*,' I quipped, taking it all in.

'Just wait till you see all the food that's been donated,' Dad replied, opening a large larder heaving with crisps, chocolates, bags of pasta, tins, cakes – everything you can imagine.

It was overwhelming to see how generous people had been.

'That's not all,' Dad continued, 'this long shelf here is where we put all the tray bakes, lasagnes and casseroles that people drop off for the families to eat. It was a godsend in those early days when we didn't have time

to cook anything. People are so kind. We're still getting food dropped off on our doorstep at home now.'

It was so humbling for me to see that my family were being so well looked after and that there was so much generosity in the world. That's not all. The JustGiving page my Dad had set up for the Royal Manchester Children's Hospital had nearly reached £10,000. This hospital was providing so much hope for families; I knew it'd be put to good use.

The next day, I got another boost of positivity when Mum and I were reunited with our cocker spaniel Milo for the first time since being in hospital. He was waiting for us in the small grassy park outside Ronald McDonald House with Georgia. As Mum wheeled me towards him, I thought he'd come running up to me, tail wagging, like an emotional scene from *Long Lost Family* – but instead he just jumped on Dad! Mum was close to tears as she gave him a huge hug, and with the sun shining down on us, we sat and ate a picnic from M&S – just like I'd dreamed of doing a week earlier. It was the first time in four weeks we were all together as a family – and made me even more desperate and determined to go home.

'We have a present for you,' Vicky said, holding a 'quad stick' – a four-pronged walking stick with tennis balls on the end. It reminded me of the cane the character Old Carl Fredrickson uses in the children's film *Up*.

'Cool!' I said, eyes lighting up, looking forward to trying it out. I still had the heavy boots on my legs, and the frame on my arm, so walking wasn't easy, but my sturdy new walking companion definitely helped with my balance, eliminating the fear that I was about to topple over.

With my physios on hand either side of me, pushing me on, I walked past my bed and attempted the one hundred metres or so down the corridor running along the front of the bays.

It was really tiring the first few times – I'd manage around a quarter of the corridor before feeling exhausted. But I kept persevering, and over the next couple of days I would attempt 'the walk' around two to three times a day – every time taking more steps without breaks.

Towards the end of the first week, I felt stronger, more confident, and actually managed to hobble along the full length of the corridor.

'Wow! Well done!' Vicky and Charlotte cheered, their faces lighting up.

'We're absolutely amazed by the speed of her progress,' Vicky beamed at Mum, Dad and Georgia as they watched me on the sidelines like proud parents at school sports day.

One challenge conquered, I was about to face another. Once I'd got back to my bay, feeling a bit hot and sticky after my walking efforts, Mum cast her eye over to the bathroom opposite. 'Do you want

a shower?' she asked. My instinctive reaction was to say 'No', but gutsy Freya who'd just walked down the corridor knew I needed to say 'Yes'.

'I don't know,' I replied, 'I feel scared. What if I get my frame wet?'

Out of all my injuries, the external fixator required the most amount of care. The pin sites had to be kept meticulously clean and dry to prevent infection, so getting it wet could put me at risk.

'Don't worry, I'll be extra careful not to get it wet,' Mum said.

I didn't tell Mum, but I was also scared about seeing the scars on my body – being confronted with the state of my face had been bad enough, I wasn't sure how I'd cope with seeing all of me. Since being in hospital, it was like I had two voices on my shoulder, one full of all my fears, and the other telling me to be strong.

This time, I decided to listen to the latter.

'OK, let's try having a shower,' I said to Mum. So, I took my little four-pronged walking stick to the other side of the ward and went in the washroom. Mum helped me undress, and then I sat on the shower chair, whilst she washed me with different shampoos and shower gels. After weeks of being cleaned with wet wipes in my bed, the sensation of the hot water running through my hair and on my skin, and the smell of fruity bubbles, felt so nice. I closed my eyes, focusing on the moment, not looking at my scars.

Afterwards, as Georgia dried my hair, she asked me if I'd felt self-conscious having Mum wash me.

'Any teenage girl would feel embarrassed,' she said.

But in that moment, I really didn't care. It was like my perspective had completely changed – what right did I have to be embarrassed about Mum helping me, when Nell's mum had lost her daughter, and countless other parents had lost their children too?

Nell's funeral was taking place in a few days' time, and though I was desperate to go and say goodbye, the doctors had said that I wasn't well enough to attend. I was devastated, but Georgia had offered to stand up and say a few words on my behalf, to which Nell's parents had very kindly agreed. I can't describe how much it meant to me that my quiet, reserved sister, who hated talking in public, was prepared to make a speech for me in front of a thousand people under such difficult and heartbreaking circumstances.

As I looked up at the ceiling that night, my freshly washed hair creating a comforting blanket around me, I thought about what I wanted to say.

'I'm sorry I can't be there,' I whispered into the darkness. 'But you'll always be here with me.'

CHAPTER TWENTY-TWO
Progress

Although I was making good progress with my physical recovery, I knew that the emotional scars were going to take a long time to heal. Along with the sadness of Nell's funeral, I'd come to hear about the London Bridge attack which had taken place shortly after the Manchester bomb. At the time, my parents had tried their best to shield me from it, but here on an open ward, where even the most hushed conversations could be overheard, it was hard to keep anything a secret. It was frightening to know that another senseless act of violence had taken place less than a month after the concert. My heart ached for all the innocent people who'd been injured and lost their lives. These days, I knew only too well how cruelly life could change in a fraction of a second.

On the same day I heard about the London attack – and as if by fate – Clare, the policewoman who was

with me on the night of May 22nd, came to visit. Her arrival was a much-needed beacon of light. We chatted about how on the night Clare was doing everything in her power to keep me awake.

'I remember you asking me about Ariana's hair and at the time I'd thought, why is she asking me such irrelevant questions?' I confessed.

'It's a police trick,' Clare chuckled. 'If you make someone stressed, then it helps to keep them awake.'

As she talked, it amazed me how people in the emergency services could stay so calm when faced with the most harrowing situations. She was yet another person who I would be eternally grateful for.

After she left, the emotional ups and downs continued when one of my nurses came by with some big news.

'As you're eating so well now, we can take the feeding tube out.'

My catheter had been taken out the day before and both felt like such huge milestones in my recovery. But the actual removal of the feeding tube was quite horrendous. As the nurse stood in front of me, I could feel the tube being pulled out from my stomach, up the back of my throat and then through my nose.

'Never again,' I said, trying not to look at the slippery tangle in the nurse's hands. Still, after my nerves had settled, I realised it was such a relief that it was gone – the tube had not only been uncomfortable, but also a nagging reminder of how sick I was.

Though I still couldn't bear to look at myself, Mum, Dad and Georgia all said I looked so much better without it.

Things carried on looking up when Jo, Angela and Martin from the dental team took impressions for my implants. We'd had a previous blow when they'd told me I'd have to wait until I was eighteen to start dental work – the thought of having to wait for four years whilst already feeling self-conscious about my new body had been really upsetting. But the dental surgeon had a daughter a similar age to me, and understood how difficult it would be for a teenager to wait that long so he changed his mind. The reconstruction work would start after I had been discharged from hospital, probably in the autumn, though a date hadn't been fixed yet.

We all felt so grateful for them for being so understanding. Coping with facial scars, especially with social media putting so much pressure on young people to look flawlessly selfie-ready at all times, was going to be hard.

And when three of my teachers, Mrs Goulding, Miss Brown and Mr Redford, came to visit me at the end of the day, it highlighted how self-conscious I felt. I didn't want them to see me like this, scarred, weak, wheelchair-bound. But of course they treated me just like they always had, cracking jokes, and before long, I started to relax.

We talked about what was happening in class, and though it was nice to see them, it was a heartbreaking

reminder that my drama lessons would never be the same again without Nell.

If I was struggling with her death, I couldn't begin to imagine what her family must be going through. My thoughts were with them, always.

The next day, on 27 June, just over a month after the attack, I woke up to the day of Nell's funeral. I felt so guilty that I couldn't be there, but as Mum and Dad kissed me goodbye to meet Georgia at the church, they reassured me that everyone understood.

'No one thinks badly of you,' Dad said, squeezing my hand before they left.

Mum's best friend, Amanda, who'd been with Mum on the night of the attack, came to look after me while they were away, along with my grandma and grandad. She'd kindly picked up a tub of M&S country vegetable soup (which had become my new favourite thing to eat), and fed it to me as I told her how proud I was of Georgia doing the speech for me.

After lunch, I tried my best to distract myself by showing off my new walking skills with my crutch. Amanda talked to me lots, doing her best to take my mind off it too, but in the back of my head I really wanted to be at the funeral. I felt like everyone else was saying goodbye to Nell and I couldn't.

I counted down the minutes until my parents came back.

They walked in, shaky on their feet, eyes red and puffy.

'How did it go?' I asked, desperate to hear about what happened, to feel like I was part of it somehow.

'It was a really nice ceremony,' Mum said. There was a tremble in her voice as she took hold of my hand. 'Everyone wore bright colours and the men had pink ties on. There were incredible eulogies from Nell's family and friends and the number of people who attended was amazing – hundreds – lining the churchyard. It was raining so they were all huddled under umbrellas, listening to the service on loudspeakers.'

'Oh, and Ed Sheeran sent the family flowers,' Dad added. 'Her brother Sam mentioned it during the service.'

This made me glow inside as Nell loved his music.

'I wonder if they were from Tesco's,' I quipped, making a wry reference to one of his songs, 'Supermarket Flowers'.

Mum placed a small white booklet on my lap. I peered at it. On the front was a beautiful picture of Nell smiling, in her stylish glasses and with her dark brown hair fanned around her face, the words: 'A Celebration for the life of Nell. 16th April 2003 – 22nd May 2017' underneath.

I started to cry, filled with a mixture of emotions. I was so happy that she'd had such a beautiful service, surrounded by all her loved ones, remembering her for the kind, caring, loving person that she was.

'Georgia did so well,' Mum said, softly, as if she was reading my mind. 'She managed to stay so composed while reading out your speech.'

And I'd meant every word I had written: 'I think that the strength and bravery that I have now was passed on from Nell, because I always admired her courage and determination in life.'

CHAPTER TWENTY-THREE
Positive Vibes

It was time to finish the eight-point plan so I could go home. The previous month had been a rollercoaster ride both physically and emotionally, but no matter how many corkscrews, loop the loops or sheer drops my body and mind had been through, I could now see the end of the track. I leaned on the words Georgia had so kindly spoken for me at Nell's funeral – that I could draw strength and bravery from Nell.

First things first, I needed to keep eating, so I asked Mum and Dad if we could go to the hospital café for breakfast. I spotted a can of Red Bull and thought that might help power me up. I'd never had it before, and afterwards I felt completely pumped. Back on the ward, I walked 300 metres with just the aid of the crutch.

'Go, Freya!' laughed Vicky. 'We can try the stairs tomorrow.'

The downside of all the action was that my arm was left very sore, but I was pleased with my progress.

'Can I have one of those German sweets?' I said to Dad, grinning. He looked at me, rolling his eyes.

The previous night a large, heavy shoe box, wrapped in ribbon, was delivered to the ward with an address from someone we didn't know in Germany. Dad immediately freaked out, grabbed the parcel and headed out of the ward with it as Mum and I looked at each other, confused.

About an hour later, he came back, holding the box, looking sheepish. He confessed that he had thought it might be an explosive device and had taken it to two police officers to open safely.

'And?' I asked, 'What was inside?'

'These,' he replied, showing me the open box.

Inside, it was full of packets of German sweets with lots of little notes and a letter filled with kind messages.

I giggled at Dad, feeling the Lewis family dark sense of humour rising to the surface for the first time.

'Dad, you're an idiot,' I said. 'Not so much Bomb Bomb as Bon Bon!'

Mum and Georgia burst out laughing behind their hands, as Dad smiled at me, half-sheepish, half-impressed with my joke.

Ever since I was little, I can always remember us using humour to help us through difficult situations. 'If you don't laugh, you'll cry,' Dad used to say. And

I had cried enough for now. I needed to be strong, I needed to keep going.

The next morning, the positive vibes continued, when Vicky and Charlotte helped me tackle some stairs. They took me to this unusual room on the ward with stairs leading up to nothing.

I still had my astronaut-style boots on and between them and the giant frame on my arm – really too much weight for my tiny frame – my legs felt like they didn't belong to me, but my crutch had given me a lot more confidence. Flanked by Charlotte and Vicky like two bodyguards, I struggled my way to the top. I was so happy, I felt like I'd climbed a mountain – maybe not Everest, but a good Snowdon, I'd say. Afterwards, they trained my parents to help me when we got home.

Back at my bay, I popped the 'Stair Assessment' Velcro label on my Harry Styles Chart to mark that I'd completed it, feeling one step closer to home.

Nurses Beth and Jenny came by the ward to see how I was doing.

I hadn't seen them for a while, so they were amazed to see me up and about.

'Look at you!' Jenny said, her voice breaking with emotion.

I'd come a long way from the weak, nervous girl who could barely move or eat in the High Dependency Unit.

As well as my nurses, I had a surprise visit from Phil and Kim, the couple who helped me on the night

of the bombing and who stayed with me until I was reunited with Dad. There are no words to express our gratitude to these people, who I reached out to and who helped me, even when they didn't know that their own daughter and granddaughter were safe. They spent well over an hour with us, and it meant to so much to me that they were able to see how far I had come on my road to recovery, when the last image they had was when I was seriously injured and in pain. Kindness, I realised, had been my medicine too.

All of this bolstered me, and pushed me to complete my longest walk yet outside, which meant I only had one more step from the physios to go – getting in and out of the car – before I could go home.

We were in Ronald McDonald House, having lunch, when the senior matron came to find us, her cheeks flushed with excitement. 'Prince Charles and Camilla are coming to the town hall and Camilla would like to meet some families from the attack. Would you like to go?' A couple of weeks earlier, Prince William had visited the hospital and Mum and Dad had met with him, but I was due to head into surgery and they didn't want to stay longer than shaking his hand. (Mum had also worried that she looked a mess and that Dad had been in his jogging bottoms and slippers.) How many people get a second opportunity to meet royalty?! We all looked at each other, and gave an enthusiastic 'Yes!'

It was all set up for 1.30 p.m., but I had a flurry of appointments to get through, so by the time we were ready to go it was 1.50 p.m.. A taxi came to pick us up – one of those large ones that open up fully at the back with a ramp – and before I really knew what was going on, the driver just bounced me up into it while I clung on for dear life. We were hurtled through the streets of Manchester, to the back entrance of the Town Hall (which is a building grand enough to rival the Houses of Parliament, if you've never seen it before) to avoid the gathered paparazzi. Surrounded by security, we were ushered into a massive room with fancy canapés and coffee, and Mum wheeled me to the window so that I could look out over the city. It was nice to see it all standing proudly: beautiful redbrick buildings next to shiny high rises, the streets that crisscrossed between them bustling with cars and people and life.

Around twenty minutes later, the Duchess of Cornwall came in with her entourage and sat down on one of the elegant sofas. She was warm, chatty and smiley, telling us all about her niece, Emma Parker-Bowles, who had recently been in the perilous reality TV show, *The Jump*. She thought it was madness that Emma had participated in these challenges where so many celebrities had been injured before. We were laughing about this, and then Dad moved on to some shady territory which I thought was about to get us thrown out.

He was talking about how we had been hounded by the press with reporters turning up at the door, following Georgia from school, leaving letters on the doormat and calling Dad's phone.

'Of course, you've seen the worst of it too,' Dad remarked, referring to Princess Diana. 'It's 50/50 who we hate the most – the media or ISIS.'

Mum and I both gawked at Dad, thinking that this wasn't the time or place to be displaying his dark sense of humour.

But then Camilla gave a diplomatic chuckle, and I breathed a sigh of relief. We chatted some more, with Camilla inviting us to Clarence House, and then around half an hour later she said Prince Charles would really like to meet us.

Whilst we'd been talking with Camilla, he'd been doing press interviews with the mayor, but then he appeared. He was smaller than I'd imagined, looking very regal in a navy blue suit.

'Nick said something really funny about ISIS,' Camilla said to Prince Charles, and then Dad said the joke again.

He laughed, and then talked about his uncle Lord Mountbatten, who had been killed by an IRA bomb – from his tone, it was clear he personally understood the devastating impact of terrorism.

After around an hour, it was time to say our good-byes and we made our way back to the hospital. My

neck was in agony from being upright in the wheelchair for so long, but it had been so worth it. Being back in Manchester, the city we loved, had been such a big lift, and whilst I'd never had many opinions on the Royal Family before, we couldn't help but admire the support they had given us. It was such an honour to meet them – a surreal experience I will never forget.

CHAPTER TWENTY-FOUR
Time to Go Home

After my brief taste of the outside world, I was even more determined to go home, and speculation was rife about when that might be. It wasn't just a case of conquering my physio chart, we also had to get the sign-off from the various departments and medical teams, collect all the drugs I'd need and make sure our home was adapted with handrails, a hospital bed and a shower seat amongst other bits. After a full-on day with two physio sessions, Dad wheeled me down to my new happy place – the Lavender Room – to chill out. It had purple walls and sofas and the calming scent of lavender in the air. I kept thinking that Nell would love this room as lavender is Ariana's favourite colour. I'd come here a few times now, one of the most memorable being with my acting teachers, Jenny and Lee. I remember we were sat on the purple sofas and Lee launched into an emotional conversation about

losing two of his sisters in just ten weeks, followed by his dad soon after.

'So, I understand your pain,' he said, looking at me with sad eyes, hugging the leather jacket he always wore closer around himself. 'It's going to be hard, you may need counselling.'

I remember seeing my parents and Jenny exchanging 'Should-he-really-be-telling-her-this?' glances, but I drank it all in. Lee had that look of every villain in every film, but, along with Jenny and her cool mop of wild curly hair, he was the nicest human.

In that moment, I knew he got it – the pain, the heartbreak.

Through their acting classes, they'd both taught me the importance of expressing myself and being open. So, now, as I found myself sat here again in the Lavender Room, I had a hankering to speak with my schoolfriend Elliot.

He was close to Nell – the three of us would often sit together in History – and had messaged me his number, saying that he was here if I ever wanted to talk. I found myself pressing dial.

'Hello?' his familiar voice filled my ear.

'Let there be light!' I giggled back.

'Oh God, I'm never going to live that down, am I?' he sighed.

Hearing his voice transported me back to the time he made Nell and me crack up during a History exam. We

were all sitting silently completing the paper, when the teacher said to Elliot, 'Can you please open the blinds? It's getting dark in here.' He replied, 'Yes, sure. Let there be light!' and yanked on the blinds so hard they all tumbled down! The teacher was furious, instructing him to 'Sit back down immediately', and, spluttering into our papers, Nell and I wouldn't shut up about it for weeks. Every time we saw him we'd say, 'Let there be light!' Now, as we reminisced about school, I felt so happy to be chatting with a friend of Nell's. Over the hour, he filled me in on what was happening in Holmes Chapel: new couples, what subjects people had picked for their GCSEs, any dramas. It was another connection to where I was heading, and it felt so good.

After we finished talking, I turned to Dad and said: 'Right, I want to do the last step – I want to get in the car tonight.'

'OK!' he replied, jumping up from the purple sofa.

He brought his car round to the front of the hospital, and wheeled me all the way down to the entrance. I got out my little crutch and with pure determination, I somehow got into the car.

I remember sitting there and saying to Dad half-jokingly, 'Come on, let's go!' I was so desperate to leave at that point.

Back on the ward, the final step was ticked off my poster. And as if by fate, that night my form tutor, Ms Barbara Morris-Brown, came to visit. Dad had

told me that whilst I'd been in the HDU she had been delivering food to all the nurses, and when she walked in with one of her trademark floral kimonos fanning out behind her and a big smile on her face, I realised how much I'd missed her.

She was laden with gifts from my classmates, including postcards filled with generous handwritten messages about how everyone at home was thinking about me. 'These are for you,' she said, handing me a fluffy teddy and a little angel figurine. 'We had sports day recently and everyone ran with pictures of you on their backs.'

'Really?' I replied, eyes wide, shocked by the level of support for me back at school.

'Of course,' she smiled. 'Everyone is so eager to find out how you are. They come to tutor first thing in the morning and anxiously ask me if there's any news. I read out your Dad's blog updates.'

I was deeply touched by how much everyone cared. In the back of my mind, I had fleeting worries that they must hate me, thinking how did I survive when Nell hadn't.

The next day, whilst we waited to hear about whether I could go home or not, I decided to go the arts room with the play leader Casey, who, every day, would walk up and down the ward, trying to encourage patients to leave behind the mundanity of their bays

and get lost in a colourful world of arts and crafts. I sat painting a banner for Georgia, congratulating her for passing her driving test. She'd passed it first time just the day before, which was unbelievable considering the difficult circumstances. This was the first time I had written anything since the attack, and as I gripped the paintbrush in my stiff fingers and dipped it slowly in the glitter paint, it made me realise that I was incredibly lucky that it wasn't my right hand that was injured.

All the while, I was feeling really achy and tired but tried to tell myself that I was OK.

Dad came to see me and said, 'You aren't looking too good,' and suddenly I was overwhelmed with nausea and went white.

'I need to get back to the ward now,' I said and as soon as I got into bed I started throwing up violently. I'd recently been put on these horrendous-tasting milkshakes to help boost my energy, and they clearly didn't agree with me.

Simon Brown, the Associate Hospital Director, came running over with a sick bowl.

'Tilt your head forward,' he said gently, his nurse's training kicking in. Although he now managed the hospital, he was so down-to-earth, always walking around the wards checking up on the patients. During our time in hospital, he came to find us literally every day that he was there, and in many cases helped sort

out problems we were having. Now this was the last
– and biggest – of them all.

'Don't worry, we will get you home today,' he said,
looking at me with kind eyes. In the meantime, all these
surgeons came around to release me, and started specu-
lating about whether I was well enough to go home.

'I'm fine, I'm fine,' I kept insisting. All my stuff was
packed up – I was bursting to go.

I sat, waiting in my wheelchair the way that our dog
Milo stands at the front door when he wants a walk, until
about 8 p.m., refusing to be floored by this last hurdle.

Then, a member of the medical team came over and
said, 'We've got everything for you,' and handed my
Dad bags of drugs so large that it was as if he was
going home from the supermarket laden with Bags for
Life – ironic really, as they literally were.

Mum and Dad quickly jumped up and went to load
up the car, then hurtled back to get me.

'Ready?' Mum said, breathing heavily from running
around the hospital.

'Yes!' I shouted.

Before we left, I said my heartfelt goodbyes to
everyone on the ward, feeling pangs of guilt that I
was leaving them behind, and went to see all of my
nurses. Seeing everyone gathered around me, the team
who had helped piece me back together, bit by bit,
was so incredibly overwhelming and I started to cry
as they hugged me and wished me well.

When I had come into the hospital five and a half weeks ago, I was broken and burned, twenty-nine injuries shattering my body from head to toe. The impact of the attack had been so catastrophic that doctors had feared that I would be left brain-damaged. But now I could walk and eat again, my wounds were on the mend, my bones regrowing. These people had made it all possible.

'See you soon,' they chorused, standing in the corridor and waving me off until I disappeared out of the double doors. Mum, Dad and Georgia helped me out of the hospital toward the car. I couldn't stop smiling: I was finally going home! It was a moment which had once seemed impossible. We reached the car and encountered our first solo hurdle – Dad struggling to help me sit down in the front seat. We were conscious not to knock my frame, and I thought, 'This is how nervous new parents must feel when they take their baby home from hospital for the first time.'

As we drove off, I looked back at the hospital, experiencing a jumble of emotions. I was so happy to be returning to Holmes Chapel, but I'd be lying if I didn't admit that I also felt nervous. I was leaving behind the safe cocoon of the hospital with all its incredible nurses and doctors who'd worked tirelessly to look after me, to this new world full of uncertainty. As the streets of Manchester whizzed by, people seemingly going about their everyday lives, I closed my eyes and thought about our 'new normal'.

PART THREE

PART THREE

CHAPTER TWENTY-FIVE

Bed

Coming back home was a very quiet affair. As much as I wanted to see everyone, I knew that I'd need time to settle in, so Dad had refrained from updating the blog to avoid a stampede of people at the door.

As we pulled into the driveway, our neighbours, Mhairi and Geoff, came over with Milo.

'Hello!' they smiled, giving me a careful hug. 'Welcome home, the street hasn't been the same without you.'

As we chatted, I noticed two tubs of beautiful red pansies placed on either side of the doorstep.

'These are so pretty,' I said.

'I know,' Mum replied, smiling. 'Someone had left them for us after the night of the attack. These two have been watering them for us while we've been in hospital.' Mum nodded at our neighbours, who beamed back at us.

I'd only been back a few moments, but already I felt like I was being hugged by the warm embrace of our small community.

I slowly shuffled into the living room with my crutch, to see that my godmother had hung up a 'welcome home' banner for me. Whilst I eased myself down into one of our big leather armchairs, Mum set up all my cards and gave me little presents that people had dropped around. Honestly, it had been like Christmas for over a month, the amount of gifts I'd been showered with; and every time I was given a new one, I still couldn't believe the overwhelming generosity I'd been shown. As I looked at my presents in wonder, Dad desperately tried to keep an excitable Milo from jumping on me, terrified he would knock my arm or legs.

I sat there, tired, dazed – and a little scared. How had I not noticed it before? Yes home was warm and cosy and comforting, but it was also a veritable DANGER ZONE. I was terrified about knocking my arm or falling over, knowing that nurses wouldn't be there to jump into action if something were to happen, and my eyes scanned the room, clocking all the things I could potentially trip on or bang into: rug, TV, coffee table, a toy Milo had dropped. I told Mum the house needed to be Freya-proofed, like I was a baby who'd just started crawling, and she laughed.

I sat there for around an hour, just soaking up the familiar smell of the place and the feel of it, and then

my eyelids started to droop. 'I'm so tired,' I said to Mum and Dad. 'I think I need to go to sleep now.' With my parents either side of me, just like Vicky and Charlotte had showed them in the hospital, they helped me up the steps. I had my right hand free so I could hold on to the bannister, but I was still so wobbly on my feet, and eventually Mum and Dad had to pretty much carry me up.

This was the most steps I'd tackled in one go, and by the time we reached the top, we were all exhausted – if the steps at the hospital were Snowdon, I really had now scaled Everest.

As Mum and Dad helped me into my room, the first thing I noticed were my pink walls. The joy at being home was suddenly engulfed in a wave of sadness. It had been the background to the video I had filmed with Nell whilst we'd got ready for the concert, telling the camera how excited we were. I forced my eyes to look away from the walls, settling on the bed instead. It was covered in my trusty One Direction duvet cover which I'd had for years: the wave receded a little.

The occupational therapists had already kitted out the house with specialist equipment for me, with a frame around the toilet to help give me support when I went to the bathroom and handrails and a chair in the shower. It was weird – I thought I'd feel more independent being at home, but in some ways it made me realise how helpless I still was as now it was my

family who had to do everything for me. Mum helped me wriggle into fresh pyjamas, while Dad fiddled with the controls on the hospital bed in my room, getting to grips with how to make it go up and down.

'Right, let's get you in then,' he said, and they both helped me get comfortable, adjusting the raised sides so that they wouldn't knock against my frame.

'It's so much better having this bed,' I said with a little smile, my head sinking into the pillow. 'At least I won't fall out in the middle of the night!' Mum looked at me, eyes watering, suddenly overcome with emotion.

'It's so good to have you home,' she whispered, kissing me on the forehead.

At the time, I didn't realise the gravity of this moment for Mum. On the night of the concert, knowing I'd be home late, she had laid out my pyjamas on the bed and hung up my school uniform ready for the next morning. Then, she received the call from Dad to say I was in hospital, and had rushed out the door, everything remaining untouched. A couple of days later, whilst I was in the operating theatre, Mum had left the hospital to lay flowers at the school for Nell. She'd come by the house to pick up a few bits first, and stumbled numbly into my room. She saw the pyjamas and school uniform, untouched, and it hit her like a sledgehammer what had happened.

Full of heartache, she'd then gone to the school to meet Georgia, who was helping to organise the flowers,

and Tony, the school's business manager, who was handling all the press enquiries. After she'd laid down the bouquet, along with a small card she'd written on my behalf, Tony had taken her to a room they had set up for Nell with messages and pictures of her, and the horrifying reality of the situation hit her all over again. In a daze, she'd returned to the hospital, with no idea whether I would ever sleep in my bed again.

CHAPTER TWENTY-SIX

Tough Love

Having an injured child at home changed the whole routine of family life. After the night of 22 May, we all knew that things were never going to be the same again – it was impossible – but I don't think any of us could imagine how much life would change.

Before, we were an active family and were always here, there and everywhere. At the weekend, we'd pick a park to go to with a nice coffee spot and take Milo for a long walk. But now we were all stuck at home, with me – this big baby – who was dependent on Mum, Dad and Georgia for everything. I had to have a cocktail of painkillers in me even before I could attempt to get out of bed. When I woke in the mornings, I'd give Mum and Dad a shout, then they'd come in with this little pot rattling with pills and a big glass of water for me to wash them down with – I was surprised I didn't rattle myself afterwards. After that, it was a collective

effort to get me ready. My parents were terrified of hurting me, mostly because of my frame, and treated me like a delicate china doll.

The hospital had a shower in a wetroom. Our bathroom wasn't designed to be a wetroom, but it turned into one every morning after trying to get me washed – it'd take well over an hour and we'd use every towel in the house. It was absolute carnage – but it could also be quite funny. I remember one time, Mum had just finished helping me shower when she needed a hand getting me out. She turned around to tell Dad, who'd been on standby the whole time, only to find an empty Dad-sized spot next to her.

'Where've you gone?' she shouted.

'I've gone to get a dry T-shirt!' Dad's voice drifted down the hall.

For some reason, this tickled me immensely – I think it was the sheer ridiculousness of Dad getting so thoroughly soaked that he'd needed to change his clothes. Of course that set Mum and Dad off and we all ended up laughing uncontrollably – we'd learned by now that, even in draining and difficult situations, there was always some light relief to be found.

After shower duties, Mum would carefully massage my scars with creams and oils as she'd been shown how to do whilst I was in Burns. I'd had steroid injections put in my hands to bring the burns down, but they'd still take a long time to fade and heal.

After I was dressed, it was time to navigate the precarious stairs, then I'd walk to the armchair with my crutch, where I lived for the rest of the day until it was time to make the mountainous journey back up the stairs to go to bed. During the daytimes, slumped in my chair, I'd watch endless hours of TV, usually shows tinged with nostalgia as they brought me the most comfort. Georgia was on school holidays, and she and I re-watched *Hannah Montana*, making me feel like I was seven again, while Mum and I caught up on all the *Corrie* that we'd missed in hospital. Knowing we were huge soap fans, my drama teacher had very kindly contacted ITV, who gave her the whole box set and she'd dropped it over – yet another example of the kindness we'd experienced.

In between TV binges, Dad had his first full day back at work, and nurses would come by every other day to clean the pin sites of my frame which was still as painful as ever and something which I wished I'd left behind in hospital. But, as with everything so far, there was someone close by to make things seem a little better. My Auntie Bev had ingeniously adapted the tops of my pyjamas by cutting the left sleeve and then attaching Velcro straps so that they would fit nicely over my nine pins.

* * *

I'd done my best to avoid looking at my scars, but around three days into being at home, I'd woken up

to a beautiful summer's day and felt really hot. 'Do you want to pop some shorts on?' Mum asked. 'We need to take off your boots today anyway to let your skin breathe for a bit, it might feel nice for you to have some air on your legs.'

I remember sitting on the edge of the bed, and looking down at my bare sausage legs, bright red from all the cuts, wounds and burns. Despite their angry appearance, in that moment it didn't really sink in that they were proper scars.

'They'll disappear at some point,' I kept telling myself.

The injuries on my face weren't so easy to escape. Mum would wash my hair every other day, and as she carefully dried it, I'd snatch a glance of myself in the mirror, not very closely, but enough to see that the left-hand side of my face was still covered in black dots – tiny fragments of metal shrapnel on the surface of my skin. It reminded me that the left side of my body had been the unlucky side; the side that had been facing the bomb when it went off. Then there were my scars; one under my eye, and the biggie at my mouth. There was also one stretching across my neck, shaped like a cherry-lipped smile, which I hadn't noticed until I'd got home. It had been caused by the string of the sports bag I'd been carrying on my shoulder with my Ariana merchandise inside, which had jammed around my neck during the explosion. I couldn't help but feel like a badly drawn cartoon character. Desperate to

cover them up once I got the go-ahead from my skin clinic, I became obsessed with looking at YouTube videos of make-up tutorials on how to conceal scars in preparation. I had a little cushion which my parents would prop underneath my iPad so that I could watch them without straining my neck as it was so still so sore and stiff from the whiplash.

However, on my fourth day of being at home, my cosy routine of watching TV and YouTube all day got a shake-up when my new physio came round.

She walked in dressed in a smart black and white physio uniform whilst I was sat in my new favourite spot in the armchair.

'Hello, I'm Carol,' she said, bright blonde hair framing a stern-looking face.

'Now, let's see you get up.'

I was momentarily shocked, taken aback by her brisk, direct manner. 'Uh . . . OK,' I stammered, grabbing hold of my crutch.

I wobbled to my feet, Mum hovering in the background to catch me.

'No, you stay there, Mum,' Carol said, firmly. 'Freya needs to learn to do this on her own.'

Mum looked equally shocked but, to be honest, we needed some tough love. Mum was always on hand to help – whether it was pushing at my back to help me stand, or keeping a steady grip on my arm as I walked along. I needed to learn to do it for myself.

After I shuffled around the living room with my crutch, Carol then said, 'Let's go to the stairs and you can show me how you get up.'

We gathered at the bottom of the staircase.

'Give me the crutch,' Carol said.

Me, Mum and Dad all looked at one another, terrified.

'What?' I said. 'I can't do that!'

'You can do it,' Carol urged.

Trembling, I put my right hand on the railing, and glanced nervously at my parents. Mum was on the verge of tears.

I struggled to go up – my legs weren't used to having so much pressure on them, and I still had the heavy boots on.

It took me around three minutes before I managed three steps, but somehow I'd done it. It was a small achievement, but it felt like a victory.

Coming back down, I felt like my knees were about to buckle.

'I'm not sure how I did that,' I panted, catching my breath.

'I told you you could do it,' Carol smiled.

Within two days, she was making me walk from my armchair across the living room to the conservatory without my crutch, adding on another couple of steps every day.

The weight of my frame pulled me down on one side, so it was really hard not to fall over, but Carol was strict

– she wasn't taking no for an answer, especially when it came to the most terrifying exercise of all; balancing and bouncing on a huge yoga ball in the middle of floor. I was worried I'd roll off onto my arm, but she insisted that it was important to develop a strong core, and with my friends coming to see me for the first time at the weekend, I wanted to be strong for them.

When Saturday came around, I was so excited, though Mum said they could only stay for forty-five minutes as she knew how tired I would get. It was a really warm day, and Mum wheeled me out into the garden. Sitting in the sunshine, I felt strangely relaxed. In lots of ways, it just seemed like a normal Saturday catch-up with my mates. There were eight of them, and they all trooped in with big smiles and bags of gifts, which I was not expecting. They well and truly spoiled me with a personalised Build-a-Bear which, when you squeezed its paw, said: 'We love you so much, Freya. Get better soon.' They'd also bought me a beautiful silver Tiffany necklace engraved with my initials and a load of Reese's chocolates, my favourites. 'You really shouldn't have got me all this,' I said, completely over-whelmed. 'I don't deserve it.'

'Yes, you do! We've all missed you so much,' they said. 'Everyone is rooting for you at school.'

I wasn't sure whether they would want to talk about the attack, but then they just came out and asked me what I remembered from the night.

It didn't faze me at all, and I told them how I remembered everything, that I was conscious until I got to hospital, and that I saw my arm hanging off. I wanted to be open with them, not hold back, but then I started to worry as they were all sat looking at me in silence, with these sad expressions on their faces, which made me feel sad that I'd upset them so much. As I was talking, in my head, I just kept thinking, 'Oh my God, look at their faces.' I had clearly shocked them a lot.

Afterwards, I decided to lighten the mood, reminiscing about funny things which had happened at school and telling them about inappropriate jokes Dad and I had made in hospital. (I'll never forget the time he mistook a woman's baby for Alfie the Pug – 'It was from a distance!' he kept saying in his defence.) We ended talking about Nell, remembering her, saying how much we missed her, and by the time the forty-five minutes was over, I was so exhausted, I went back to my chair and fell fast asleep.

CHAPTER TWENTY-SEVEN

With the Good Comes the Bad

The start of the second week at home brought with it the worst bout of sickness I have ever experienced. Out of the blue, my body had got completely fed up of the barrage of drugs I was on and as soon as I took them, I'd throw them back up again.

I couldn't keep anything down, not even a single garden pea (that's not an exaggeration) and was vomiting around four times a day. By the third day, I was looking so awful Mum anxiously called the doctor and asked for an urgent home visit.

He checked my stomach, and prescribed an anti-sickness drug which was available at a chemist ten miles away that closed in twenty minutes.

By this point, Mum had gone to see Georgia perform with her orchestra, so Dad had no choice but to shove me in the car, and speed through the windy lanes of Cheshire, just about managing to get there (and keep

my stomach down) before the doors shut. I took the anti-sickness tablets for three days and was still so ill. Some days I couldn't even wake up because I felt so terrible. Mum, who'd never let me have a day off school sick, was determined to continue my physio, and would still try and get me to walk around a couple of times a day.

One afternoon, she walked me to the end of the garden, where I was violently ill and Georgia had to run to me with a bucket into which I threw up all the antibiotics and tablets that were jumbling around. That was one of my worst periods – I'd sit there crying, feeling ill, drained, empty, shivery, icky.

In and amongst all this, I was still having regular appointments and check-ups under all my various departments as an outpatient. Around a week into this horrible bout of sickness, we received a much-needed lift when my lead surgeon Matt Nixon told that us the breakages to my legs – the broken tibia in my left leg and fractured ankle on my right – were healing nicely and that I could lose the boots soon. It was such a relief as they were so heavy, although it meant that I'd have to start learning to walk again without my boots on – but after all I'd been through I decided it could only be a cinch in comparison.

The sickness eventually got so bad that, a week later, we went back to the hospital. The doctors decided to take me off all the drugs apart from the painkillers.

It was a risk as the antibiotics were crucial in helping to prevent the spread of infections – but incredibly, throughout my journey so far, I'd not had an infection despite all the surgery, open wounds and fractures, burns, physio, pin cleaning, shrapnel in my eye and everything else. 'It's a miracle,' the doctors had told me, and I was beginning to realise that it really was.

CHAPTER TWENTY-EIGHT
Therapy

After two weeks at home, I was getting fed up of watching TV and had started to sit in the conservatory, looking out over the garden full of colourful summer blooms. Seeing my friends had made me reflect a lot about Nell and everything that had happened. Being at home, away from the distractions of check-ups, X-rays and surgeries, I had a lot more space and time to think, and this is when I really started to process the events of May 22nd.

I've always loved writing – and had been given lots of beautiful new notebooks whilst I was in hospital – so I'd sit in one of our padded beige garden chairs and release my thoughts on paper. I wrote a poem for Nell, my memories about being in hospital and my worries about the future. I'd also sit and look at old pictures and videos of my beautiful friend. The last video I had of her was on my phone, taken at the concert. Nell was

singing at the top of her voice, very badly. I thought I'd lost that special moment for ever as, on the night of the attack, my phone had been flung from my hands. But, unbelievably, the police had not only managed to find it, but with the Harry Styles case still intact. As I played the video, I smiled at the memory – my gorgeous Nell didn't have a care in the world, and I loved her even more for it. The conservatory became like a therapy room for me.

It was almost time for me to give the speech I'd promised I would give to the school on the last day of term. I cast my mind back to when I'd first pledged to do this in the HDU, how I'd worried so much about how everyone at school was feeling, consumed with guilt that I wasn't there to grieve with them for Nell. I'd wanted to let them know that I was OK, and that I was still there for everyone else – and having seen my schoolfriends recently, my compulsion to make the speech had become even stronger. Saying that, I was still terrified. The last time most of them had seen me was when was Nell and I were bouncing around the school full of excitement about going to the concert – we left the two of us, and only one of us was coming back; and I worried about their reactions.

Though my writing was coming along, the physical act of it was still a struggle – tiring and time-consuming – so Dad and Georgia sat down with me in the conservatory and I dictated to them what I wanted to say.

On the day, Mum helped me dress in a nice red top customised with the Velcro straps – 'We might see these in London Fashion Week,' I joked – with a pair of stretchy leggings. As much as I loved my skinny jeans, they were still a no-go. She then tried to straighten my hair, but it was so weak and damaged; I kept seeing strands fall away and flutter before my eyes. 'Don't worry, it'll get stronger again,' Mum said, sensing me tense up. The hairdressers who'd painstakingly washed my hair in hospital had kindly given me thickening and strengthening shampoos to use; a small gesture which had meant so much.

I used a finger on my right hand to carefully pop my contact lenses in again for the first time since my eye surgery, and I was finally ready.

It was pouring with rain, so Mum, Dad and Georgia had to make a dash with me in the wheelchair to the back of the school, where we were met by Tony, the school business manager. Since May 22nd, he'd become a real source of support for my family and he greeted us with a big smile.

'Hello, Freya,' he said, his face lighting up when he saw me. 'It's so good to have you back again.'

'Thank you,' I smiled weakly, a jumble of nerves. I'd been here a million times before, but the red-brick, white-windowed buildings suddenly felt very unfamiliar, as if they belonged to someone else. We followed him to the doors of the assembly hall and

waited outside. Looking down at my sheets of paper, I felt sick but I didn't tell anyone.

'Are you ready now?' Tony said.

I gave a small nod and Georgia wheeled me inside. I was expecting everyone to be standing up cheering – usually the case when someone gave a talk at school – but I was met with a sea of faces sat looking at me as they applauded in an oddly muted way. One of the teachers handed me a small microphone, and my sister stood by me with the sheet as I read out the words . . .

'I've missed you so much. I've been through a very long, hard and painful journey the past couple of months but I wouldn't have gotten through it without the support this school has given me. I want to thank you for all the lovely cards, gifts and messages you have given me. They were truly uplifting and made me happier each and every day.

'As you can see, I've got a fair amount of wounds, but the most painful thing was discovering I'd lost one of my best friends. The loss of Nell still doesn't feel real and I'm sure for me and many of you it won't do for many years to come. Nell Jones was the nicest and most down-to-earth girl I had ever met and I feel so privileged to have called her my friend. I will and always will think of her every day.

'During my time in hospital, it was amazing to hear about how much this school came together. Like lots

of people say, good things always come from a bad situation and everyone supporting each other is definitely one of them. My family played a big part in my recovery. I've become closer to my wonderful parents as they sat by my side every step of the way and I won't ever be able to thank them enough. I also couldn't have gotten anywhere without my incredible sister, who has now become my best friend.

'Let's have a toast even though we don't have any glasses. A toast to Nell, an amazing girl that'll never be forgotten. A toast to me on my final road to normality. And a toast to Holmes Chapel Comprehensive School, becoming a family.'

As I said the final word, everyone was in tears and I started to cry too. Afterwards, Georgia wheeled me to the side so that I could watch the rest of assembly, but I was conscious of the room half-looking at me, and couldn't help but feel a little like an animal at the zoo.

After assembly, Georgia pushed me to my tutor room where my classmates had gathered to say hello.

'Why was it so quiet in there?' I asked.

'The headteacher told everyone not to cheer,' she replied. 'They didn't want the loud noise to scare you.'

I wasn't sure whether to laugh or cry at this. On the one hand it was so considerate of them, but on the other, it made me scared that I'd always be treated differently from now on.

Going to see my tutor group was also strange and exacerbated that worry a bit, but I tried to put it down to the fact that I was visiting, and that it would be different when I came back for good. My schoolfriends formed an orderly queue and came and hugged me one by one, as if I were a bride at a wedding (only without a groom). With my left arm out of action, I couldn't really hug them back so I just sat there.

It was difficult to face everyone, but it was something I felt compelled to do. You see, out of my friendship circle, I'd always been the agony aunt, the one that people turned to when they were feeling down. I've always loved to make other people feel better. To me, there is no greater feeling. Even when I was little, I'd make cards and write letters to Mum, telling her how much I loved her and how beautiful I thought she was – she still has every one tucked away in a box in her room. So, I wanted to show everyone that I was still there for them, even if internally it was a real struggle.

After tutor group, we went to the headteacher's office to meet my teachers. Passing through school felt really weird as I'd see places where Nell used to hang out. *That's her bench,* I thought to myself as we went past a seating area outside reception at the front of the school. By the time we got to the office, I was really upset but desperately trying to hold it together, reminding myself that I was lucky to be the one of us still here.

*

Afterwards, I was exhausted and emotional. It was so nice to see everyone, but I was worried that they wouldn't know how to talk to me any more. I was so lucky to be back there, but heartbroken to know Nell would never be.

I looked at my phone and saw that it was pinging with messages from my classmates saying how brave I was, and how much they had missed me. It was like a weight lifted off my shoulders. I reminded myself that actually I'd done an amazing thing: I'd been so afraid to show my new face and body but I'd done it anyway; I'd been so scared that they wouldn't want me back, but they didn't hate me after all. I had conquered my fears and it felt like I had really turned a corner.

CHAPTER TWENTY-NINE

Shopping

It was a bright, sunny Saturday, with light flooding in through the window casting dancing shadows on the carpet. We were all sat in the living room, Mum and Dad chatting amongst themselves, when I looked outside and piped up, 'Can we go out for lunch today?'

'What?!' they replied, shocked.

'Yeah, it's a beautiful day, I really fancy getting out the house.'

Apart from giving the speech in school, this was the first time I'd expressed a desire to venture outside voluntarily, and it was an opportunity Mum and Dad weren't going to pass up. They sprung out of their seats quicker than a jack-in-the-box, and helped me into the car with Georgia in tow.

We headed to the local shopping centre to a new Costa coffee which did the best pesto, mozzarella and tomato paninis. As we weaved through the shoppers, I sat in the

wheelchair, a blanket draped over my legs, feeling self-conscious, scared that people were looking at me, judging me, but in actual fact everyone was just going about their business – of course they were. I soon relaxed, and we settled into the Costa. My mouth was watering by the time Dad came laden with a tray filled with coffees and toasted sandwiches. At this point, I still couldn't eat anything hard, and could only chew at the back of my mouth, but I swallowed down the self-consciousness, as it felt so good to be out for lunch with my family like normal.

This moment really kick-started my appetite and I started thinking about all the foods I wanted to eat.

'Can we go to Tesco's after this?' I said to Mum and Dad. 'And Next? I fancy having a look around if that's OK.' My parents were so happy for us to be out together that I think I could have asked them to drop me at the tattoo parlour to get a Manchester Bee inked on my arm and they would have agreed.*

In Next, Georgia pushed me around the clothes aisles as I picked out comfortable long-sleeved tops and floaty trousers to cover up my scarred arms and legs. Into the basket also went a brown leather shoulder bag to replace the one I'd lost in the attack.

Making our way to the checkout, I spotted a shimmering turquoise and blue sequinned sleeveless mini dress on the sales rail. It reminded me of the sort of thing

* Dad says no way would this have happened.

Hannah Montana would wear on stage, and on impulse I asked if I could buy it. 'I'd like to wear it when I appear on *The Ellen Show*.' Georgia and I are obsessed with the famous American chat show hosted by comedian Ellen DeGeneres, and at some point in hospital, probably when I was lying awake at night with my thoughts, I'd decided that one day I'd go on there and tell my story. Now I had the perfect dress for the occasion . . .

Laden with shopping bags, we then went to Tesco's and loaded up on my Italian favourites: spaghetti and tagliatelle. Georgia was pushing me along when we both spotted a pizza oven and started fantasising how amazing it would be to make fresh pizzas at home.

'Can we have this?' we asked Mum and Dad.

'No!' came the reply.

We begged and begged, until eventually Dad ended up carrying it out of the supermarket.

On our way back to the car, we went past a row of shops that Nell and I had been looking at just a couple of months earlier when we'd gone shopping for the concert. I suddenly felt really teary thinking about how happy and excited we'd been. I remember us going to the Boots opposite and checking out the make-up aisle. Nell had picked up an eyebrow palette and examined it closely.

'This would be perfect for you,' she'd said. I didn't buy it at the time, but now I felt an overwhelming need to have it as it would make me feel closer to her.

'Actually, can we go to Boots?' I said to Mum. 'There's something important I need to get.'

Back home, we all collapsed and messily ate pizza made with our new kitchen gadget, strings of mozzarella sticking to our fingers. Through tired eyes, I looked at all my new things, the eyebrow palette being the most special of all.

It was retail therapy in the true sense of the word – everything I'd bought represented my road to recovery and gave me something to work towards, whether it was having the confidence to wear a sleeveless dress again or being able to use my fingers to put on make-up. It was the first time I'd allowed myself to look to the future, a hope which had been nurtured by the incredible love and support I'd received, not just from my loved ones but complete strangers. Dad was back to updating the blog with my progress, and our JustGiving page had already reached a phenomenal £17,000.

It was the cherry on the cake to a dream day and I went to sleep smiling.

CHAPTER THIRTY
Stumbling Block

The positivity continued when, shortly afterwards, X-rays revealed that the bone in my left arm had grown back enough to remove the cumbersome metal frame which had been attached to me for the last ten weeks. This was my first surgery since coming home, but as I arrived at the hospital, I was calm. It all felt so familiar: the hospital gown, the little anaesthetic room. It was my fourteenth operation to date so I was used to it by now.

I woke up and, through the grogginess, realised that I couldn't feel my arm. I blearily looked over to my left side, and my fleeting happiness at seeing the frame gone was snatched away by the sight of a huge white cast instead.

I became aware that Mum and Dad, who'd resumed their old positions next to my bed, were talking to the surgeon.

When he saw me looking at him, he came closer.

'Hello, Freya,' he said. 'The good news is the frame is off. The bad news is . . . '

He then explained that when they took the frame off, they had manipulated my arm to see if it was strong enough. They'd bent my arm the tiniest bit and it snapped, like a bent lollipop stick.

'What?' I muttered, which by now had become the most used word in my vocabulary.

Once the fog over my brain had cleared, it hit me what had happened. My arm had broken – again – and now I'd have to wear this cast for another two months. Luckily I was able to go home that night, but I was in agony.

I woke up the next day and lay in bed, crying, as every time I moved my arm, excruciating pain shot through my limb. Basically, there was still a gap in my arm where my weak bone had come away, with only a sliver of bone holding it together – which is why it had to be so heavily bandaged.

It took my poor parents two hours to sit me up in bed, there were tears everywhere, and I wished they hadn't taken my frame off.

The irony is that just the day before, my boots had been officially removed – marking a huge step in my road to recovery. But now one cast had just been replaced by another. I remember walking across to the bathroom on my weak, wobbly legs and all of a sudden

I was engulfed by so much pain that everything went blurry and I fainted. Luckily, my parents were there to catch me, but I felt sorry for them: how much more of this did they have to take?

The next two weeks passed in a dark fog of pain and sleep, struggling to be positive as, lying there housebound, it felt like I'd taken a giant leap backwards.

CHAPTER THIRTY-ONE
Dedication

Behind the scenes, Georgia, who had by now established herself as the best big sister in the entire world, had been working on ways to get my spirits up. She'd posted on Facebook asking for help getting hold of tickets for Harry Styles's BBC live show on 30 August. And, in yet another act of unbelievable generosity, we ended up with five tickets – three from a friend from the village, and two from a complete stranger who'd responded to her appeal on social media.

'Guess what?' Georgia said, flopping down next to me on the sofa in the living room.

'What?' I asked, grumpily.

'Guess who's going to see Harry Styles . . . ?'

My mouth fell open.

'You are joking?' I stammered.

'Am I the best sister in the world or what?'

'Yes! Yes! Yes! I love you!'

In that moment, it didn't even occur to me how I might feel being back in the atmosphere of a concert again. All that was on my mind was that I was going to see my one true love.

Leading up to the concert, the pain in my arm started to ease, and I was walking more and more unaided. Carol had ramped up my training, holding sessions in her treatment centre in the village. She'd do a lot of massage on my neck as the whiplash was causing me so much pain, and she warned me that I might find it difficult at the concert as I'd be sat in my wheelchair for so long.

Two days before, I'd finally been given the go-ahead from the skin clinic to start wearing make-up again, so we went on a family shopping trip to the department store. I'd spent ages researching on the internet the best brands for covering scars and, after reading rave reviews, decided to try out Kat Von D. We headed to the counter and told the beauty consultant about my situation. Her eyes watered as she listened to my story, and she very kindly spent ages with us, telling us about the best products to use, and how to apply them.

I came home laden with a bagful of concealers, foundations and powders to cover my scars – it reminded me of the bag Dad had been given at the hospital with all my pills but, for me, this make-up was now my medication.

The formulas were very different from the base I was used to wearing – school only allowed a very light tinted

moisturizer, but these products were creamy, thick and full coverage. So, a life hack: if you ever get a scar, put concealer on first, then powder, and then another layer of concealer – and that helps to offer the most coverage. For me, I had to put on six layers before I was happy to go out. I know it sounds like a lot, but formulas nowadays are so advanced, super buildable and natural without looking caked on.

On the day of Harry's gig, Georgia helped me to apply the make-up as the fingers on my right hand were still quite weak. Mum and Dad had bought me a new jumper for the occasion – a baggy pink sweatshirt decorated with all of Harry's tattoos. I was over the moon. I'd been begging for it for months, but Mum and Dad had refused on the grounds that they'd never spend their money on something so 'hideous' – but being the lovely parents they are, they eventually gave in and now here I was, wearing it. Or attempting to.

It was a struggle to get it on over my cast, and in the end my neck was aching from tussling with it for so long. However, now that my boots were off, I could wear jeans for the first time, which felt like a small win.

It used to take me an hour or so to leave the house for a big event, so even by my standards it had taken me for ever to get ready, but finally after a good few hours of hard graft we were ready to leave. We had a spare ticket, so one of my friends, Amy, came along

with us. We got there for 3 p.m., and the security guard looked at me, smiling.

'Nice jumper,' she said.

Dad, being the painfully honest guy that he is, replied, 'We paid £60 for it, which we wouldn't have done if it wasn't for what happened to us,' and told the security guard our story.

'Oh my God,' she said, and started crying. 'Wait here, I'll be back.'

A few moments later, she came back with Harry's personal security guard. 'Hello,' he said, 'Harry would really like to meet you.'

I couldn't believe what was happening. I was wearing Georgia's smartwatch, and my heart rate was hammering at 158 beats a minute as we were led backstage, where we met Harry's two guitarists, Mitch and Adam. The security guard introduced us, and they gave me a kiss on the cheek.

'Harry's got a few new ones now,' Adam said, nodding at my jumper. I was feeling so emotional and overwhelmed that all I could do was peer at him through my lashes and smile at him meekly.

'Harry will be here in a sec.'

The moment I heard those words, I couldn't stop crying.

My parents, sister and Amy all tried to calm me down.

'You need to stop,' they said. 'You'll make yourself sick.' But then Harry walked in and I couldn't breathe.

He looked a vision in a black bomber jacket, black skinny jeans and brown boots.

'Hi,' he said, bending down to give me a gentle hug.

I turned to Dad.

'Can I get out of the wheelchair?' I asked, nervously.

'Sure,' Dad replied.

And with that, I got out, leaped forward and basically flattened Harry. I held on to him with my right arm, not wanting to let go. I'd dreamed about this moment for so long, thinking that if I ever got to meet him properly, I'd tell him all the things I loved about him, but as I drank in the smell of his aftershave, I was so overcome with emotion that I couldn't say a single word.

After we hugged, he started chatting to Amy and me about school, and then asked if we were coming to see him in concert in November.

'No, we didn't manage to get tickets,' I replied.

'Don't worry, we'll sort that out,' he said.

Dad then stepped in, and told him about how I'd started singing his song 'Sign of the Times' in the back of the ambulance when I thought I was about to die. Tears rolled down his cheeks, he was so touched, and quite lost for words. Looking around, I realised that everyone there was crying.

I remembered that Nell had always said that if I ever met him, I must get a photo of him kissing me on the cheek. I was too shy to ask Harry, so I whispered my request in Dad's ear and he passed on the message.

'Yeah, of course,' Harry replied, and we posed for the camera.

Even though I still didn't like having my picture taken, it was such a happy moment, and I knew that Nell would feel so proud of me for getting the snap of him.

After around ten minutes, it was time for Harry to get ready for the concert. We wished him luck and said our goodbyes while I internally berated myself for not getting a grip and talking to him properly. We went and took up our positions close to the stage, and shortly afterwards, Harry came on and started to perform.

Halfway through, my neck started hurting beyond belief and I struggled to hold it up, feeling like a baby with a floppy head.

Seeing me wince, Mum kept saying in her worried tone, 'We can go if you like?' but there was absolutely no way on earth I was leaving, so I used all my strength to push through.

Toward the end of the set, Harry announced that he was going to sing 'Sign of the Times'.

'I want to dedicate this song to somebody who is in the audience tonight,' he said.

His mum was behind us, so I thought he was going to dedicate it to her, but then he went on to say, 'She is a really special friend to me, she is sat over there. Freya, this one's for you.'

I burst out crying once again and so did everyone else. As I listened to the lyrics, thinking about how far

I'd come from that moment in the ambulance, it felt unreal. I got lost in the moment, appreciating every word that he sang.

This whole time my parents were worried that I'd be terrified to be back at a concert, but one of the things I love the most about being at a gig is that you get lost in your own world. When I was there, I wasn't worried for myself at all, but what I did feel was sad; so sad for Nell – and her family – that she'd never be able to enjoy a concert again.

After the set finished, Harry's mum started chatting with me.

'I bet he feels really glad that he met you,' she smiled, bending down to give me a hug. 'We have to stick together, you and I.'

She had recently lost her partner, and I think she understood what I was going through.

We eventually got home at 1 a.m, and I collapsed in to bed, my body secretly wracked in pain. I woke in the morning barely being able to move my neck, but I still felt on cloud nine.

CHAPTER THIRTY-TWO

Back to School

After I'd recovered from the drama of the Harry Styles concert, I started preparing to go back to school, which signified a huge step forwards in my recovery. Thanks to my sessions with Carol, I was becoming more confident walking around without my wheelchair; not for miles and miles, but enough to be able to get to lessons.

The day before I was due to go back, Mum, Dad and I went to school to chat with the teachers about my return. They were really understanding, suggesting giving me a pass so that I could leave lessons and go to lunch five minutes early to avoid my arm getting bashed in the crowds. I also had a little pass if I was feeling upset or wanted to talk. I just had to show it to my teacher and they would ring up Student Services, who'd come and get me, like my very own 'Get Out of Jail Free' card.

Mum and Dad came away feeling really reassured, and though I was also touched by the effort they were making, I must admit, I had mixed feelings. On the one hand, I wanted people to acknowledge what had happened, but on the other, I didn't want special treatment. My biggest worry, however, was how I'd cope without Nell being there. In the time before, I'd meet her every day in the morning, and give her a hug. I always felt safe at school as she was always there. It was disconcerting knowing that she wouldn't be.

Shortly before I was due to start school, our family liaison officer, Dave, emailed to say that he thought they had found the tan brown bag I had lost on the night of the attack. A few days later, he popped over, carrying a shoe box. We all sat down in the living room, and I slowly opened the lid.

There, wrapped in tissue paper, was my bag.

It'd obviously been cleaned, as it didn't have a mark on it, the smooth, polished leather giving no clue of the damage and destruction which had been caused that night. I opened it, and gasped. Inside, there still lay my glasses case with a neatly folded-up five-pound note tucked away inside. Nestled next to it was the red MAC lipstick I'd bought on that shopping trip with Nell especially for the night – the one which, with one slick of her artful hand, had made me feel so grown-up.

'Thank you,' I said to the Family Liaison officer, my voice thick with gratitude.

Later that evening, I took the bag upstairs and went to place the red lipstick on my shelf along with some others. I suddenly had a flashback to the concert. I remembered getting it out for a re-touch and Nell had asked, 'Can I use some too?' 'Of course,' I'd replied, handing it to her. She dabbed some on her lips and smiled. Now, as I looked at the lipstick in my hands, I realised that it contained a small part of her and I vowed never to use it again. As I prepared to go back to school, it seemed like she had sent me a sign that she would always be by my side.

On my first day back, I woke at 6.40 a.m., giving myself an extra forty-five minutes to get ready in the morning. Usually, I'd just throw on my school uniform, do two quick plaits and apply a bit of lip gloss. But, today, Mum helped to conceal my white cast under my shirt and school jumper and then I carefully put my make-up on. I looked in the mirror, wincing, my scars staring back at me, as I painstakingly applied layers of concealer, trying to hide them away. Before May 22nd, make-up had been something I'd really loved and had fun with – my friends would always ask me to do their eyeshadow for parties, and I had a plastic filing cabinet filled with hundreds of products and brushes. Now make-up felt like a necessity: my armour.

The doorbell went and I heard a cheery 'Hello!' at the door and thudding up the stairs. One of my friends had kindly offered to come over before school and do

my hair for me, weaving it into a beautiful French plait. By 8.30 a.m., I was finally ready to go. A few more friends came knocking at the door and we all walked to school together just like usual, as Mum stood at the doorway waving us off, tears in her eyes, watching me toddle off down the street. It'd been her goal to get me to school, but one which she never thought would actually happen.

As we neared the gates, I felt a knot in my stomach. I had a vision, like in those American teen movies, where I'd walk in and everyone around me would stop talking and stare. It echoed the time that I was wheeled into the school assembly at the start of summer when everyone just looked at me, in silence, and I had thought, *Is this what my life is going to be like from now on?* But, when I walked into the school yard, apart from a few people coming over to give me a hug, no one really paid much attention. I had braced myself for people asking me questions about the attack, which I felt confident I'd be able to answer without getting upset, but worried how they would deal with the answers. In my head, I had imagined that they'd ask me what I remembered, and what it had been like to be in hospital for so long. I feared that everyone would know exactly what had happened to me and they'd treat me like the girl in the Manchester Bomb attack and not Freya. But, as it happened, the day passed relatively uneventfully.

My friends were trying not to make a fuss but at the same time they were tiptoeing around me.

When I walked to the usual spot where we always had lunch, they said, 'Do you want to sit here? Everyone get up for Freya!' which made me laugh.

'It's OK,' I joked, 'I won't break.'

Leading up to the attack, there had been a lot of arguing within my friendship group. I guess it's maybe something which happens in lots of teenage friendships, but it had caused some sadness and loneliness. Things were different now – my whole perspective on life had changed – and I wasn't going to watch it happen any more.

'I don't want us to argue any more,' I told everyone, 'life is too short.'

'We don't want to argue either,' they replied.

We all hugged, and cried, promising to value one another and our friendships. It was a precious thing, and something that has become clearer and clearer to me since the attack: from now on I always want to show people and be vocal about how much they mean to me.

Throughout that first day, I knew Mum would be camped anxiously by the phone, waiting for a call from my tutor, Ms Barbara Morris-Brown (or BMB as we call her now), asking her to pick me up after a couple of hours. My parents were convinced that I'd

only be able to manage half a day, but remarkably I lasted the whole of it, which surprised me too. I think my determination to get back to normal again pushed me on along with the support from my amazing tutor.

Since the attack, BMB and I had formed an incredible bond and as the weeks went on, she would become my own personal cheerleader, bolstering me with her life lessons and kind words of encouragement. If it wasn't for her, I don't think I would have been able to go back to school full-time. There aren't enough words to express my gratitude for everything she has done for me.

But, back to that first day, by the time I stumbled back through the front door, I was exhausted and pretty much fell asleep on the sofa before poor Mum had a chance to ask me how it went. But, as first days back after a near-death experience go, I thought it had gone pretty well.

CHAPTER THIRTY-THREE

Love

Life isn't straightforward. When something bad happens in movies, things always get better. There's probably a stumble, but by the time the credits roll, the line on the graph is only heading in an upwards direction. Reality is different. The line goes up and down, up and down, especially when mental health is involved. It's not very nice, but we have to accept that it's part and parcel of recovery.

It was at the start of the second week back at school that things unravelled a little. I was in tutor group (a daily catch-up on the school's news) when my teacher handed me my old music exercise book. I flipped it open and everything zoned out around me. The first thing I saw was Nell's handwriting saying 'Freya and Nell's recording piece', and I burst into tears. Music was one of our favourite classes together, and I was teaching Nell how to play piano when she'd written

this. The whole tutor group was looking at me. The teacher asked everyone to leave and then sat with me until Georgia came. I was inconsolable. All I could think about was that I'd never have music with Nell again. After that, memories of Nell would consume me suddenly, without warning, completely knocking me sideways.

During one RE lesson, I remember walking into the room, sitting in my seat, and everything, and everyone, around me going blank. It felt like when you're daydreaming and you can hear people talking around you, but you're lost in your own world. There was a guy sat opposite me, but in my head, I went back to when Nell sat there – it was like an out-of-body experience where I was watching Nell chatting and laughing away. I tried to push it to the back of my mind, but it wasn't easy, and I was left feeling incredibly shaken. I didn't tell anyone in class as I didn't want to draw attention to myself, but when I got home, I told my parents and Georgia everything. They were my rocks, and if it wasn't for them, I don't know how I would have coped.

Over the following weeks, there were many more episodes like this. But, the hardest was when I sat down in class to do 'five-minute reading', an initiative the school had started to encourage us to read more fiction by starting each lesson with a few minutes of quiet time with a book of our choice. I'd gone to

WHSmith's and picked up a new book, and flipped it open at the start of class.

The words began dancing in front of my eyes as I suddenly remembered that a couple of weeks before the attack, Nell had read exactly the same book and we'd had a conversation about it. There's a chapter where the protagonist talks about her friend who died, and she lists all the things she'd never get the chance to do.

'Imagine never being able to get married or have kids or do your dream job or not even finish high school,' Nell had said, her eyes filled with sadness. 'Well, obviously that's never going to happen,' I'd replied, trying to reassure her, 'but imagine how awful that would be for other people.'

Now, I sat in class, staring at my book, the conversation playing over and over in my mind. I kept quiet the whole lesson, lost in my inner turmoil, and then got home, opened the door, and burst into tears. I cried to Mum for hours, as I remembered how Nell had told me how she never wanted to miss anything out of her life. I thought about all these things she'd never have the chance to do, and for weeks afterwards, I'd go around school and feel almost angry that life was going on whilst Nell wasn't here any more. It was really difficult, but I kept these feelings to myself. I felt like no one else could really understand what I was going through.

Then, one day, I was walking home from school when a car drove past me with a sticker on the back saying, 'Pray for Freya, we miss her'. I turned to my friend and said, 'Does that say my name?'

'Yes,' she replied. 'There's loads of them going around.'

I looked at her, stunned. After that, I began to notice the stickers everywhere. It was as if, every time I started feeling down, the universe held its hand out to me to make me feel better. When I ventured into the village to do my next physio session, I noticed bee stickers stuck everywhere too – in shop windows, on lampposts and car bumpers. Since I was little, I'd known that the bee has been a long-standing symbol of Manchester, but Dad explained that after the attack, the bee had taken on an extra special significance, being used as an emblem of unity and love.

I remembered that when I was in hospital, a few of the nurses, including Beth, had new bee tattoos inked on themselves. Back then, I'd been overwhelmed by the outpouring of support I'd received, but it was only now that I was out in the real world, and my mind wasn't so numb from the shock, drugs and surgery, that I was really beginning to understand the true scale of the support that was out there for everyone whose lives had been impacted by the attack.

Mum and Dad felt it was the right time to show me some of the press coverage in the wake of attack – and showed me videos and news articles of the floral tributes

which had been left in St Anne's Square in Manchester to honour the victims. I was moved to tears as I saw, for the first time, the dramatic images of the colourful sea of bouquets, balloons, toys and cards and read that the square had become a place of pilgrimage for tens of thousands of people who wished to pay their respects and express their sympathy to the dead and injured. I hope this doesn't sound like I thought all of these tributes were for me, but seeing the outpouring of affection made me feel so loved.

These feelings intensified when, shortly after, I heard that a special garden at the school was going to be created in memory of Nell. Donations had already started flooding in via the Remembering Nell Foundation which had been set up by Nell's family. The leadership team at school had meetings with me and Nell's closest friends to look at the plans and help with the design.

One of the elements I loved the most was 'the river of pebbles' where people could paint a pebble with their own personal tributes to Nell to form a colourful meandering 'river' through the garden. I thought about what I wanted to write on mine, then while I was at home, listening to one of our favourite Ariana songs, 'Moonlight', the lyrics touched my heart.

'I never knew you could hold moonlight in your hands till the night I found you.'

Tears streaming down my cheeks, I knew they were the perfect words to express how I felt.

Over the following months, people from all walks of life, from neighbouring schools to local businesses, pulled together to make the memorial a reality. People fundraised, donated flowers and building materials, volunteered to dig patches and plant shrubs. As I walked into school every day, it was incredible to see the garden taking shape like a peaceful sanctuary. I had no idea that Holmes Chapel had such a strong sense of community, full of so much compassion, warmth and kindness, qualities which embodied the very spirit of Nell, and which I vowed to carry forward too. We had been the victims of the most horrific act of violence, but out of that one, terrible night had come a downpour of good. So, when there was news of another terror attack in London which saw twenty-two people injured when a bomb was partially detonated on a tube train at Parson's Green Station, I knew that I couldn't allow myself to be full of full of fear, anger and hatred – as that would mean the terrorists had won. I owed it to everyone who had rallied around me – and most of all to Nell – to carry on spreading the love which had been shown to me. It gave me strength to open up and carry on. Talking to my family and friends had become my therapy. Whenever I felt a twisted knot in my stomach forming from a sudden flashback, or tears welling in my eyes from a memory that had rushed into my consciousness, I instantly told Mum, Dad and Georgia. I've lost count of the number of times they

held me close as my tears soaked through their clothes while all my hurt and pain poured out in a cathartic rush. They listened, unflinching, an endless supply of tissues pushed into my hand as they gave me the space to express how I felt. I honestly believe that the open relationship they nurtured from when we were little, where Georgia and I could talk to them about literally anything, ended up being my sanctuary and sanity. Because of this, I haven't felt the need to have further counselling other than the sessions I had in the hospital, but that may change one day, and that is OK.

CHAPTER THIRTY-FOUR
Getting on with it

Despite making strides, physically and mentally, it was becoming apparent that not all my injuries were healing so swiftly or certainly, and there was lasting damage I'd have to learn to cope with. X-rays showed my left arm was healing well, and I could start to remove my arm brace for long periods of time, though it was still safer for me to wear it at school. However, I had very little feeling and movement in two of my fingers on my left hand. I'd first noticed a problem when I was in the Burns Unit. After the bandages had been taken off my fingers, and the physio started working with them, it felt like the little finger on my left hand wasn't responding. Medics realised that a nerve had been ripped when the bone had been taken from my arm. At the time, the doctors had been hopeful that the feeling would return. Now, although the nerve seemed to be gradually recovering, nobody knew how long it

would take until I had full movement and sensation back. This meant I'd have to drop Music. The realisation was incredibly sad for me, as I loved music and it was one of the lessons I really enjoyed doing with Nell. I decided to study Psychology instead – a subject Nell had talked about picking – so in a way, I still felt close to her, and it appealed to my naturally nosey and inquisitive nature.

For weeks I'd also been suffering from terrible migraines – I'd had them for years and they were usually worse during periods of intense stress and concentration, enveloping me in a sudden fog of pain, so no surprise really that they'd come back with a vengeance. Carol thought that the headaches could be linked to the whiplash, and despite her intense work on my neck, I was still in a lot of discomfort. I suspected that, out of my twenty-nine physical injuries, this one would take the longest to heal.

Despite this, I woke up each day determined to get on with it. It was coming up to four months since the attack, and I knew it was a miracle that I was back at school at all. We were still trying to get used to our new normal, but I was learning to appreciate all the small wins – whether it was tying my hair back on my own for the first time or being able to walk faster.

One of the things that had given us all strength was the blog – what had started out as a convenient means for my family to keep everyone updated on my progress

had become a huge form of therapy for all us. People couldn't post comments on the blog, but they could when they made donations on the JustGiving page. On down days, we'd read all the heartfelt comments and instantly feel lifted.

They'd say things like:

'What an amazing family you are, the strength and dignity you convey and continue to share via the blog is truly inspiring!'

'No young girl should have to go through the ordeal, both mental and physical, that Freya is faced with. My admiration for Freya and her family is immense. Stay strong.'

'Your continuing story leaves me stuck for words. With love to all your family – you are truly inspirational.'

I still find it unbelievable that, from across the globe, people were following my journey and donations continued to pour in. By the four-month anniversary, our fundraising had passed £20,000, which surpassed all of our expectations and made our hearts sing. We were so grateful to everyone who had put their hands in their pockets, knowing that the money would help both patients and the wonderful staff at RMCH. They had become like a family to us, and every time I went back for appointments, I was reminded of how much kindness and compassion filled the corridors – the doctors and nurses hugging me as if I were their own child – leaving me feeling truly humbled.

My next lot of surgery was the dental reconstructive work. In October I once again found myself back in the familiar surroundings of RMCH, in the capable hands of Jo, Angela, Tamsin and Professor Yates. I also met an anaesthetist, Jan, for the first time. I'd heard a lot about her from my parents; it was Jan who had first brought me out of the induced coma. Mum and Dad had described her as crazy but wonderful, with a huge personality, and she certain fulfilled my expectations; I loved her. During the three-hour operation, they reconstructed the bone I had lost in my mouth using cow bone (which meant I was no longer a proper vegetarian, sadly) in preparation for my implants to be fitted. Afterwards, I was in so much pain. I don't think anyone could have prepared us for how swollen my face would become. My lips were so huge, they were nearly touching my nose. Halloween is a big deal in our family, and we are known for having the scariest house in Holmes Chapel, with ghosts flying across the front and sinister music playing, but this year I felt like I had my own Halloween mask on. For three days, I couldn't speak, resorting to typing stuff on my iPad if I wanted anything and barely being able to fit a straw through my mouth.

I lived on a diet of soup and water to prevent any damage to my mouth. But after the swelling went down,

I noticed that the top of my mouth didn't look so sunken and I was slowly starting to look like me again.

True to his word, Harry Styles asked his management to organise tickets for us to see him in concert at Manchester Apollo the next month. People often ask me how I can bear to go to another concert again, but it's something my family and I have enjoyed since I was little, and if I were to stop then I think that means I'd be letting the terrorist win. I can definitely feel nervous in that situation, but no matter how hard I've found it, I've been determined to keep living my life and cherishing every moment.

Once again, Harry was incredible, and I cried when he closed the evening with a 'Sign of the Times'. Every time I listened to that song, it reminded me how far I had come, how lucky I was to be here, so I made a decision.

'I think I'm going to go back to my drama group,' I told Mum, Dad and Georgia on the way home in the car.

'That's a good idea!' Mum smiled, looking back at me from the front seat.

The attack had put things into perspective – we only had one life each and I needed to make the best of mine: push myself, dream big. If I was serious about becoming an actress, then I needed to put the work in and go for it. It meant tackling one of my biggest fears, having my appearance judged.

I'd been self-conscious before, but now my insecurity about my looks had rocketed. I was so thin that it must have looked like I was a living skeleton. I tried my best to push it to the back of my mind, but I couldn't help feeling that strangers down the street were looking at me and wondering what had happened to my face. Ariana has been quoted as saying, 'Be happy with being you. Love your flaws. Own your quirks. And know that you are just as perfect as anyone else, exactly as you are.' I tried my hardest to think about that when it got too much. Then, one day, we were getting ready to go out for dinner and I pulled my leather jacket out from my wardrobe, the one I thought I'd lost at the concert, but which – miraculously – had been safely returned to me a few weeks after my bag had been found. At the time, we'd been shocked that, like the bag, there wasn't a mark on it; the leather and suede hood still perfectly intact. It was a sunny day, and holding it up to the light streaming through the kitchen window, Dad and I peered at it closely, shocked. On the jacket, in random places, were tiny tears and holes. Did I love it any less? No. I'd bought that jacket on our family holiday to Las Vegas for $80 and, I'd loved it even more, as Nell had thought it was so cool. *A few holes aren't going to stop me wearing it*, I thought, slinging it over my shoulders. It seemed to be a symbol of me now, perfectly imperfect. Like the jacket, I may be damaged, but the fact that I was still here was all that mattered.

Giving Back

At the beginning of December 2017, Georgia turned eighteen, and to celebrate her birthday we went to the Jingle Bell Ball at the London O2 Arena. In another cavernous music venue it was impossible not to draw comparisons with the Manchester Arena, but it was Georgia's day – Georgia who had been there for me in so many ways over the past six months – and, as she danced away with a big smile on her face, it was so easy to be strong for her.

During our time in London, we also went on the tube, which was packed, and shopped on Oxford Street right in the middle of the afternoon rush. I'm not going to lie, I felt incredibly nervous, internally panicking at the sight of bulky backpacks, jittery like a nervous rabbit, but I tried to be rational. Back home, we sat talking about the weekend.

'Did you feel anxious or uncomfortable in London?' Dad asked.

I shook my head: 'No'.

'The way I view the situation is simple,' I said. 'The fact that I was injured in a terrorist attack was extremely unlucky from a statistical perspective; to then be involved in another incident in my life would be beyond unlucky so, on that basis, I'm not worried.'

Mum and Dad looked at each other, a little speechless. They later told me that whilst my logic was sound, my ability to think in such a rational and unemotional way was unbelievable.

'You're a strong girl, Freya Lewis,' Mum said, proudly.

But, the fact is, my strength didn't come from inside, it came from everyone around me. As Christmas edged closer, it seemed a fitting way to end the year by giving something back to the community who'd rallied around and presenting a cheque to the RMCH from all the donations we had received via the blog so far.

Nurses Beth and Jenny, along with hospital charity coordinator, Angela, came along to a special school assembly where Georgia introduced them to the crowded hall. To a huge round of applause, we then handed over a giant cheque, the sort you see on TV quiz shows, for £24,000. It was an incredible moment – never in a million years did we think we would raise that amount of money, and we knew how invaluable it would be to the hospital, the hospital which had saved my life. It was our way of saying a massive thank you from the bottom of our hearts.

Our fundraising efforts didn't stop there. We started the New Year with a new challenge. It all came about after Angela asked Dad if he'd participate in a promotional video to encourage people to sign up to the Great Manchester Run the coming May. Dad, a keen runner, agreed straight away, and volunteered to take part in the 10k circuit himself to continue raising money for the hospital.

While Dad was pounding the pavements in preparation, my physio with Carol had reached a bit of a plateau. Her no-nonsense approach had been invaluable in my road to recovery – I could walk comfortably without needing the wheelchair on standby, go upstairs (though I still felt a bit heart-in-mouth when I went down them), do up the buttons on my school shirt and shower by myself – all things I never would have thought possible a few months ago. Through her massage therapy, she'd also discovered I had scoliosis, curvature of the spine. My lead surgeon Matt, reassured us that it could be treated with surgery, which would be scheduled once my body had got stronger. It was a setback, but I pushed it out of my mind and concentrated on the here and now. I knew that to build myself back up, I needed to do more exercise. Thing is, as you know by now, I hated PE and always had done. Remember how I froze when I clapped eyes on the hospital gym for the first time? Well, now my fear of PE had doubled as I didn't want to change in front

of my classmates and reveal my scars, so I'd stopped participating in lessons altogether.

'What shall I do?' I said to Mum, Dad and Georgia as we sat watching TV. 'I need to get more strength into my body somehow'.

'Why don't you train with that guy, Jack?' Mum said. Jack was a personal trainer with his own gym, who'd contacted us when I'd just come home from hospital. He'd heard about what had happened to me and – incredibly kindly – said that if I ever needed help with my recovery then he'd be happy to try.

'Oh yeah, that's a thought,' I replied.

I liked the idea of having a personal trainer – that way, I wouldn't have to exercise in front of lots of people and expose my scars.

Dad took my answer as a green light, and before I had time to change my mind, he was already on the phone to Jack, arranging an induction at the gym the next day after school.

We all went along, not really knowing what to expect, and I remember being quite terrified when I met him. He looked like a bodybuilder, with a full sleeve of tattoos with a giant bee in the middle and a big ginger beard. But, once we started chatting, I realised he was a big teddy bear. I told him about all about my injuries and he listened patiently. He was confident he'd be able to help build up my muscles, strength and core, and by the time he'd given me the

grand tour of all the equipment, I was booked in for my first session the following week.

To begin with, he asked me to take hold of the lightest weights and lift them over my head. 'No problem,' I replied, breathing a sigh of relief. Sounded simple enough. But, when I went to do it, my left arm wouldn't move.

We both looked at each other, shocked to realise how weak my arm was.

'OK,' Jack replied calmly. 'It's clear we need to train this arm.'

Next, we did a few sit-ups, then Jack led me to the running machine.

'This is the treadmill, say hi to it,' he said, cheekily.

I tentatively stepped on it, and Jack started it off on the slowest setting. I quickly grabbed on to the sides as it started to move, terrified that my legs would give way and I'd be flung off.

'Don't worry,' Jack said, 'You won't fall. Trust me.'

I took a few deep breaths, and willed myself to put one foot in front of the other. *It's fine*, I told myself, *it's just like walking down the road*. I managed to walk on it for around a mile and, afterwards, I felt like I was going to be sick. I remember stepping out of the gym and wasn't sure I'd even be able to make it to the car, I felt so weak.

I somehow struggled into the passenger seat.

'My legs are so weak!' I spluttered to Mum, red-faced.

The next day, my legs and arms were so sore it felt like someone had been kicking them. The same thing happened for the first couple of sessions, but slowly – slowly – my body started to get used to the exercise, and I actually managed to jog on the treadmill.

After a couple of weeks, I was attempting my arm exercises again.

Jack looked at me with a mixture of shock and pride.

'Freya, you are lifting that weight with your arm.'

I'd been so focused, I hadn't even stopped to think about what I was actually doing and, suddenly, I freaked out, nearly dropping the weight on my face! Jack was really excited by my progress and told my parents when they came to pick me up. That was a defining moment. It gave me so much confidence and made me realise that, although it was exhausting, the gym sessions were working.

Then, around the end of February, Angela asked if I'd like to be the official starter for the Great Manchester Mini Run – a 1k course for really young children. Dad, perched at his computer in the corner of the living room, glanced over at me sitting on the sofa.

'You know the Junior Run is only 2.5k . . . ' he said. 'You're doing so well at the gym. Why don't you do it?'

Before, in my exercise-hating-old-life, the idea would instantly have been thrown out the window. But now, in my new life, the thought of it didn't seem so crazy. When we'd presented the cheque to Jenny, Beth and

Angela, it had been what I thought was one of the most rewarding moments of my life. But actually finding out what the money had been spent on a few weeks later genuinely made my heart sing. It had been used to make the Critical Care Unit, the very unit where doctors had fought to save me, more comfortable for the patients and families who'd been plunged into the most desperate situations. This included new padded chairs by each bedside so that tired families, who were often sitting for hours on end anxiously waiting and hoping and praying for their poorly little ones to get better, could be comfortable during those long days on the ward; new toys in the family room so that siblings visiting a brother or sister could have a much-needed break and a new staff room for the amazing doctors and nurses whose dedication truly shone through following the attack. The money also stretched to building a laundry on the ward which allowed them to start using all the colourful bedding which had been generously donated by well-wishers after May 22nd; when we have visited since, it's been wonderful to see how this has really brightened up the unit and made it feel more homely.

I would be eternally grateful to the hospital – and the NHS – for piecing me back together. And so if running 2.5k – a mile and a half – was going to help raise more money to help more families like mine, then it was a no-brainer. 'It's a great idea!' Mum added. 'Give you a goal to work towards.'

The next day, at school, I told my friends I was doing the run.

'What?! That's amazing! But you hate running!'

I wasn't surprised by their reactions – I couldn't believe the words I was saying either. But Mum was right – it would give me a new focus, a chance to give back, and as the donations started mounting up, I was inspired to train even harder.

First, I was aiming to complete the 2.5k in forty-five minutes . . . Then it shrank down to half an hour . . . Then twenty-five minutes . . . Seeing the red flashing digits of the time on the screen getting faster and faster really kept me motivated and when I felt myself flailing, I'd think of Nell. I'm a natural worrier, and she always used to say to me, 'Get a grip!' She was a lot tougher than me, so I tried to channel her fearless, fighting spirit.

The training sessions became like a therapy for me, not just physically, but also psychologically, as Jack and I chatted about everything and anything. I'd tell him about May 22nd, Nell, music, school. I even showed him the scars on my legs. He'd listen patiently as I trained, throwing in the odd remark about my love for Harry Styles.

'Your obsession is not healthy!' he'd laugh.

'Oi! Don't be mean!' I'd laugh back.

Soon, word spread that Dad and I were doing the run, piquing media interest. The local press wanted to

interview me, and though I knew it'd be difficult to face the camera, I was determined to do it, knowing it'd be good publicity for the charity. Mum and Dad were with me, and gave the journalist a strict brief about the fact that I didn't want to talk about what I remembered from the night or my specific injuries – coming into the spotlight was a big step, and I didn't feel ready for that. My lead surgeon Matt Nixon also did an interview and, afterwards, the pledges on our JustGiving page rocketed. Before long, we had surpassed the original £24k mark – Mum, Dad, Georgia and I loved huddling around the computer and seeing the donations and messages pinging up on the screen, every word and act of kindness lighting up our lives. Soon, it had reached £30,000, then £35,000 – a generosity beyond our wildest dreams.

CHAPTER THIRTY-SIX

A Surprise

'So, girls, we have a surprise planned for you, but you'll have to take a day off school.'

It was four weeks before the run, and we were all sat around the dining table in the kitchen having lunch when Mum made this shock announcement.

'What is it?' I said, looking at Georgia suspiciously.

Mum and Dad never let us have a day off school, so I knew that something big must be up, but they were keeping tight-lipped about it. So, on the morning of Friday 27 April, we headed to the Lowry Outlet Mall in Manchester full of intrigue about what was going on. As the day progressed, we figured out that we must be meeting someone – Dad kept running off on the phone, and then coming back saying, 'They aren't ready yet!' But we had no idea who and, having looked around all the shops, Georgia and I were starting to get bored. By around 3.30 p.m., Dad announced that

our mystery meeting was running late, but that he would pay for us to have a drink at the Lime Bar, so we settled at a table, ordered mocktails and I started looking at my phone.

'Who's that?' Georgia whispered, nudging me.

I looked up and my eyes widened.

'Oh my god, it's David Platt and Shona from *Coronation Street*,' I gasped.

They were sat at the table opposite us deep in conversation. Then the street's resident baddie Pat Phelan, played by Connor McIntyre, joined them.

I couldn't believe the scene unfolding before my eyes.

'Pat Phelan's part of the scene, Pat Phelan's part of the scene,' I kept saying over and over to my family, assuming that they were doing some filming for the soap in the restaurant.

Before I could catch my breath, my favourite character Bethany Platt stormed in, her long blonde waves flying behind her.

'Stop it, stop it! You are not a murderer, you're not on the street now, all right?' she said, pointing her finger at Pat.

I honestly didn't think things could get more surreal but then Shona turned to look at me.

'Guys, it's Freya Lewis,' she said.

My mouth dropped open in disbelief as they all glanced in my direction, and started to walk towards our table.

Brandishing her mobile, Bethany Platt said, 'Can we get a picture?' and before I knew what was happening, they all gathered around me for a selfie.

'What's going on?' I stammered, as Pat smiled and hugged me, which was so weird as he plays such a convincing villain in the soap and I thought he might strangle me.

Bethany looked at me, smiling.

'Everyone at *Coronation Street* is so proud of you for the money you've raised and we were wondering if you wanted to come with us to the set?' she said.

I started to cry, disbelief mingled with joy, as Bethany gave me a big hug.

Next up, a tour of the Cobbles.

Bethany (OK, I should stop calling her Bethany now, she's actually actress Lucy Fallon) showed me around the *Corrie* set, and took me to an urban garden they had created where, in pride of place, there was a beautiful bench decorated with flowers and bees in colourful mosaic tiles.

'This bench is to remember the lives that we lost on May 22nd,' Bethany said, her eyes watering.

I welled up at the sight, knowing Nell would have loved the fact that there was a bench dedicated to her and other people at the concert on the set of *Coronation Street*.

As Lucy and I stood in the garden, suddenly Kym Marsh walked in holding a gold envelope, poker-straight hair swinging in the wind.

'Hi!' she smiled warmly, giving me what felt like my hundredth hug of the afternoon. '*Coronation Street* and Manchester are extremely proud of you. You have won an NHS Hero Award and here is an invitation and I will see you there on the night to give you your award.'

I didn't know what to say. I was just overwhelmed and felt so lucky.

'This is one of the best days of my whole life,' I said.

I was in shock in the car on the way back.

'Did that just happen?' I mumbled to Georgia, who was sitting next to me, looking equally as stunned. I realised afterwards how meticulously planned it had all been. Now it all made sense.

Whilst we were driving home, Lucy Fallon texted me, wishing me a great time at the awards and it started to sink in that something really big was happening.

By the time we got home, Mum and Dad had filled us in. A few weeks back, they'd been contacted by ITV and the *Mirror* newspaper. To mark the seventieth anniversary of the National Health Service this year, they were hosting a special awards ceremony – the NHS Heroes Awards – celebrating the country's most treasured institution and giving its extraordinary people the recognition they deserved. I couldn't believe it, but they thought *I* was one of those people.

'You've won the NHS Heroes Young Fundraiser Award,' Mum said proudly. 'We've been invited to London in two weeks' time for the awards ceremony.'

It was impossible to process the news. After seeing with my own eyes the amazing people who worked for, and supported, the NHS, why had they chosen me?! Surely I was just doing what anyone else in my position would do?

So, I asked if I could dedicate the award to Nell. She was the kindest, most caring person and wanted to join the NHS as a physiotherapist or psychotherapist – if anyone deserved to be celebrated, she did.

Once the initial shock wore off, I realised I had two weeks in which to find a dress which covered my arms and legs. It also needed to have a V-neck neckline so I could show off a special piece of jewellery. Three weeks after I'd came out of hospital, Nell's mum, Jayne, had come over to the house and given me a beautiful silver necklace with a heart. Engraved on the front was Nell's handprint and, on the back, her name.

'I'm giving this to six of Nell's closest friends,' she'd said, 'so Nell can be with you always.'

I wore it underneath my school uniform every day, so it was essential that I found a dress which displayed the necklace – then it would feel like everyone would be looking at Nell too.

After hours of searching online, I finally found a floaty full-length floral dress with long sleeves – it reminded me of something out of *A Midsummer Night's Dream* – and the moment I put it on, I felt instantly comfortable in it.

On 14 May, we all took the train down to London in the morning and arrived at the Park Lane Hilton Hotel where the ceremony was held and we'd be staying for the night. Unbeknown to us, Jack, my personal trainer, had very sweetly pulled some strings and got us upgraded to 'The Clarence Suite' – which seemed particularly fateful as Camilla had invited us to Clarence House and she was the guest of honour that night. When we walked in, I was speechless. It seemed to go on and on for ever, with a huge lounge, dining room, kitchen, two bedrooms (Mum and Dad's had a four-poster bed and a walk-in wardrobe), three bathrooms and the most spectacular views across London I had ever seen. 'This place is the size of our house,' I said, awestruck, as I whipped out my camera phone and took a video, wanting to capture this moment for ever.

The whole day was a whirlwind as we had a welcome lunch and met the other amazing winners (a truly inspiring group of doctors, nurses, health professionals, volunteers and fundraisers) and did rehearsals. A glitzy stage with big screens and a podium was set up in the grand ballroom, with elaborate chandeliers dangling from the ceiling reflecting the blue and white lighting – the colours of the NHS logo. I was still marvelling at the sheer size of the hall when they started showing us where to get on and off the stage to collect our awards. As we approached the steps, I looked out at the sea of tables and chairs dressed with pristine white

linen and floral displays ready for tonight's event, and started to panic.

'Dad, I've got heels on, and these stairs are so shiny and slippery. What if I fall over in front of all these people?'

'Don't worry, you'll be fine,' Dad reassured me.

As we were ushered to Hair and Make-up, I kept having visions of my legs turning to jelly, tripping up on the hem of my dress and falling flat in front of a roomful of celebrities. But, as soon as I started having my make-up done, my nerves started to settle. The make-up artist, Alan, was absolutely lovely. I told him how I covered my scars, and he did it the same way. After he'd finished, and my hair was styled in soft waves, I looked at myself in the mirror, something I usually hated to do. But this time, when I looked at my reflection, instead of studying my face to see how noticeable my scars were, it just felt like I was looking at me. For the first time, I didn't feel worried about facing people, which was a good thing, as next it was time for the red carpet.

All the winners, along with a host of celebrities, walked along the red carpet. It was lined with photographers, journalists and the public, jostling to catch a glimpse of the stars, including Dame Shirley Bassey, actor Michael Sheen, rapper Tinie Tempah and the stars of *EastEnders* and *Call the Midwife*. It was a windy evening, and my hair was whipping around all

over the place as I nervously made my way up with Mum, Dad and Georgia by my side, like they had always been. After a champagne reception mingling with people I'd only ever seen on television, we were all seated for dinner and the ceremony, hosted by Paul O'Grady, began.

We were sat on a table with the cast from *Coronation Street*, along with my surgeon, Matt, and nurse Jenny. The stories were all so emotional, there wasn't a dry eye in the house the entire night. Then Kym Marsh came on stage and my name was called out as a film about me started playing on a big screen. It had interviews with my family and my medical team, and as they spoke about the highs and lows of the emotional rollercoaster we'd been on over the last year, the fact that they feared I'd never walk again, the tears started to flow. I glanced around the table, and everyone was crying. I think when you see your story condensed like that, and brought to life on screen, then it really hits home, everything you've been through. I quickly tried to compose myself before walking on stage, the room filling with applause as I slowly navigated the steps.

When I got up there I was still shaking, and *Corrie*'s Lucy Fallon and Tina O'Brien, who were with me, kept giving me little words of encouragement to help calm me down. Then, before I could catch my breath, host Paul O'Grady announced that a surprise guest had come to present me with my award and out walked

Louis Tomlinson from One Direction looking HOT in a black suit and tie.

'Oh my God,' I mouthed.

He'd flown in all the way from LA for this very moment and was flying back out again immediately afterwards. He came towards me with a big smile and wrapped me in a hug as I burst into tears. I felt so special.

Holding my award, he said, 'So I just want to say, I think you are absolutely incredible. What is remarkable at such a young age is your strength, and to go through such tragedy and to raise that amount of money and have that level of endeavour is amazing. You really touched me with that story and I just want to give you another hug.'

I wasn't going to say no and I collapsed in his arms.

Ever since the attack, people had been telling me how brave I was – it hadn't felt right at all until that night, when I finally allowed myself to think, *Maybe I have achieved something significant.*

When we'd first sat down on the table, I'd noticed that there was an iPad propped up in the middle. 'What's this doing here?' I'd wondered, and picked it up. I was shocked to see it had my name on it – it was so people at the awards ceremony could donate money for the run. I showed it to Mum, Dad and Georgia, a look of amazement on my face. I can one hundred per cent say that all the support I received on that night

gave me the strength to push forward and do the run. I thought, *I've got to do it for all the people who are here tonight*. And, of course, I had to do it for Nell. With her silver handprint necklace nestled close, I felt like she was right there with me on stage, so when I was asked to say a few words, I instantly felt calm as all my feelings about Nell came tumbling out from my heart. It was a comfort being able to talk about her, and to have the chance to dedicate the award to my beautiful, kind, funny friend.

The whirlwind continued, when, the next morning, and still in a daze, we went on the ITV chat show *Lorraine*, to talk about the awards. Clips from the night were played and, as I watched it, it hit me that it had all been real.

On the train home, I thought about how lucky I was to have done all that – if you'd told me a year before that one day I'd be walking down a red carpet and meeting celebrities, it would have been a dream come true. When bad things happen, it's so easy to just concentrate on them, to feel full of anguish and heartache. But no – there had been so much good too. I took a moment to appreciate everything that had happened to me.

Before long, my phone started pinging with messages from my surprised friends. All the winners had to keep the awards a secret to prevent it leaking on social media before the ceremony happened so I'd told them I was at a hospital appointment.

'We can't believe it, Freya!' they said, forwarding newspaper articles. 'This is amazing!'

The next day, I was a couple of minutes late to school and sloped into tutor. Everyone looked at me silently and then, while I got my stuff out of my bag, one of my friends turned around in her seat with a cheeky smile and said, 'Hey, Freya? Been up to much meeting Louis Tomlinson recently?'

Everyone started giggling as I sat there blushing. I felt so privileged and humbled to have been part of the awards, and more determined than ever to get my trainers on and run my heart out.

CHAPTER THIRTY-SEVEN

A Show of Strength

Six days after the awards, I got up early, put on my green RMCH T-shirt, got in the car and we made our way to the run. When we got to Manchester, there were crowds of people and the race suddenly felt very real. It hit me that I actually had to run in front of people, and Mum had to spend a few minutes reassuring me that I wasn't going to fall over. We went over to the sign-in desk, where we met Aimee from the charity, who'd organised a chunk of the publicity that we did for the RMCH in the lead-up to the run. We'd really grown to love her, and as she placed a pair of green Humphrey Bear mascot ears onto my head, it was so nice to be able to celebrate all her hard work. I was determined to my best for her, and everyone else who had supported me on my journey, but it was also a bit overwhelming – the people, the heat – and I wondered how I was going to cope. First, though, I had to swallow

my nerves and sound the klaxon for the 1k kids' Mini Run that was taking place before mine. Georgia and I climbed onto the podium as a sea of children gathered below me. I gave them a big smile of encouragement as the air filled with a loud comedy car-honking noise and the crowd of tiny fundraisers started to toddle off down the course.

Before I knew it, it was my turn. We all gathered on the starting line and, as I looked around, I noticed that a lot of the other runners looked younger than me. With my cheeks flushing red, I couldn't help thinking, 'If they beat me, this is going to be so embarrassing.' But then I looked over and saw my friends sat on the other side of the barriers with a banner that said, 'Go Freya!' Suddenly, the klaxon went off and my immediate thought was that I was going to get trampled on, so I started to run. 'Hi, bye!' I waved to my parents and Georgia who were huddled at the side cheering me on as I went running down the hill.

As I was jogging, I spotted Clare, the policewoman, who was there with me on the night of the attack and had come to see me at the hospital. She was standing with her son, holding a colourful banner, with the cheeky slogan 'Run like you stole something!' in fluorescent pink, green and yellow letters while chanting my name, 'Freya! Freya!' Seeing them gave me a real boost, and knowing she was watching spurred me on. I made it to the 2k point before I thought, 'Oh God, I

can't breathe,' and had to stop for a second. I looked up, hands on knees, panting, as I realised that small children were running past me – so I said to myself, 'Right, Freya, you have to do this!' I thought of everyone who'd cared for me, all the messages of support on the blog, the 'Pray for Freya' stickers on people's car bumpers, the endless bags of food that had been left on our doorstep, the hundreds of gifts and cards and visitors, my family – and Nell, always Nell. I pictured her standing with my friends, screaming, 'You can do it!' and a burst of strength propelled me forwards, making me sprint uphill for the final half kilometre. Running into direct sunlight, beads of sweat trickling down my face, I thought I was going to pass out, but then I saw Clare again, clapping and whooping, and my legs kept going faster and faster.

And then I saw it. The finishing line. I ran as fast as I could as the cheers from the crowds got louder and louder and the guy over the Tannoy said, 'It's Freya Lewis here, and she's coming over the finish line!'

I crossed the line to be greeted by my family and flashing cameras. After a quick pit stop of lying on the floor because I was pretty sure I was going to throw up, I got up, gulped down lots of water, and was asked to do some interviews.

One of the reporters said, 'You couldn't walk a few months ago, and now you're running, how does that make you feel?'

All I could think of to say was, 'I haven't done anything special.'

And it was true – all I was desperate to do was to say thank you to the people who had saved me.

After the interviews wrapped up, I went over to my friends and tutor and showed them my purple medal as they all hugged me, screaming, 'You did it! You did it!'

'Not only did you do it,' Dad said, 'but you did it in seventeen minutes – your fastest time yet.'

'No way!' I squealed in shock.

I got straight on to the phone to Jack to give him the news.

'That's awesome!' he shouted down the phone.

We went back to the charity tent and were met by more congratulations and 'Well done's, and then Dad prepared for his run. He was sporting a backpack with bees on it with his water bottle tucked inside, and a pair of sunglasses with a bee design. As we cheered him on, it was such a big milestone for us as a family. We had been through the darkest time in our lives – a time which could have left us fragmented, angry, full of despair – but here we were, united, hopeful and full of love. And when Dad crossed the finishing line, grinning from ear to ear with his silly sunglasses and backpack, I felt so unbelievably proud of him. I thought of all the things he'd done for me, how much money he was helping to raise and felt so grateful that I had a family who'd do that for me and for the hospital.

Later, when we all gathered around the computer at home to look at our JustGiving page, we couldn't believe the figure staring back at us: £40,000. In two days' time, it would be the one-year anniversary of the attack – and the day our lives changed for ever. I stared at the incredible number on the screen, more money than I had ever seen, and it gave me strength to know that, out of our heartbreak, we would be giving hope to others.

CHAPTER THIRTY-EIGHT
Remembering

On the day of the anniversary of the Arena attack, I was meant to be off school, but in the morning I had an overwhelming desperation to see my friends. The guilt still hadn't left me from being unable to console them a year before, when it all first happened. I went in for the first lesson, gave my friends a big hug and then Mum, Dad, Georgia and I went to Manchester for a special memorial service at Manchester Cathedral attended by Prince William and Prime Minister Theresa May. As we listened to the service, I still don't think it had really sunk in that it had been a year since the attack. In the morning, Mum had said, 'Today will be hard for you, it will be a year without Nell.' But, in my head, I didn't see it like that. To me, it felt that Nell had been with me every step of the way. I hoped I'd embodied her fighting spirit and zest for life, and I could still hear her constantly telling me, 'Get on with it, Freya Lewis!'

I bowed my head for the two-minute silence at 2.30 p.m., touched by the quiet contemplation of the hundreds of people who had gathered in the cathedral to remember the twenty-two victims who had lost their lives and hundreds of others who had been injured. Afterwards, we all went outside, lost in reflection, and met Phil and Kim. I hadn't seen them since they had come to visit me in hospital, and I gave them each a big hug, remembering how they had helped me on the night.

We went to a cafe for lunch with Laura, another victim, and her parents Nan and Michael. Although we'd been in hospital at the same time, we'd both been so poorly that we hadn't got the chance to know one another properly, but our parents had become good friends on the ward, united in the unimaginable situation they had found themselves in that evening. It was nice to talk to another family who truly understood what we'd been through, but Laura's and my ways of dealing with May 22nd were very different. While I had found talking to be a therapy for me, Laura still found it hard to open up. And, while Laura felt comfortable with her scars, I felt deeply self-conscious about mine.

After we'd said our goodbyes, and left the cafe, I turned to Mum.

'I wish I was more confident, like Laura,' I said.

'Always remember, you are beautiful the way you are,' Mum replied, giving me a hug as we walked toward the city centre. 'You should wear your scars

like a badge of honour, they are a symbol of how far you've come, how strong you are, never forget that.'

I was thinking about Mum's words as we wandered into Primark, and started absentmindedly glancing through the aisles.

I know it might seem strange going shopping on the one-year anniversary, but I think we all wanted the day to feel as normal as possible, and looking around the shops is something I'd always loved to do. Now, of course, everything I was drawn to either had long sleeves or covered my legs. I wondered when I'd be brave like Laura and feel comfortable with my scars, wear them with pride, like Mum told me to. A woman's voice cut through my thoughts.

'Are you Freya?'

I looked up to see a kind face smiling at me.

'Yes,' I replied, confused.

'I read about you in the paper, doing that charity run. Well done! You're so brave!'

Taken aback, I smiled and mumbled a thank you.

She gave me a little hug, and then went off, waving.

'What just happened there?' I said to Mum.

But, it wasn't a one-off. Throughout the day, lots of strangers came up to me, saying similar things. By the time we arrived at St Anne's Square for a special concert – the Manchester Together – One Voice event – I was so full of love: once again, the kindness of strangers was lifting me up, a recurring theme in my life now.

The square was filled with people of all ages – families, kids, couples, pensioners. We were waiting for the music to start when I suddenly realised that the people stood in front of us were the same people who did my X-ray exactly one year ago on the night of May 22nd.

'Hello!' I said, as Dad tapped them on the shoulder.

'Freya!' they replied, faces glowing, as they gave me a hug. 'Look at you! It's so good to see you!'

Then, I turned around and saw all my friends. It seemed unbelievable, given the thousands of people who were there, that we would all be together in the same spot.

As we linked arms and sang songs, it was a poignant moment – our voices united in a joyous act of solidarity. Music had been ingrained in the history of Manchester, bringing people together from all over the world, and this night showed the spirit of the city and the true power of music. On the way home in the car, with Georgia snoring softly next to me, Mum, Dad and I kept saying, 'Has it really been a year?'

We got home, exhausted, and immediately got ready for bed. Mum and Dad were pulling the duvet over themselves when I snuck into the middle of them. The clock on their bedside said 22.31 p.m. – the exact moment the attack happened.

'Happy anniversary,' I said quietly, and Mum and Dad both gave me a hug, their eyes glistening in the moonlight.

'You are still here,' Mum said.

Cocooned in their safe embrace, I felt so lucky.

After a few minutes, I went back to my room, crawled into bed and, as I looked up at the ceiling, I thought about Nell. The tears flowed and I cried myself to sleep. For me, it would always be a day about who I'd been with when it happened, and I missed Nell so much.

CHAPTER THIRTY-NINE
With Both Hands

The NHS Heroes Awards aired on TV two days later and, after that, everything went crazy. I was sitting on the sofa with my iPad when Dad shouted over.

'Freya, do you want to speak at Westminster Abbey? They're putting on a special event to celebrate the NHS.'

He explained that a guy called Antony had got in touch. He was organising the NHS's seventieth-birthday celebrations, and after seeing me on TV was wondering if I'd like to be involved.

'OK!' I replied. Before, I would have hesitated, but now I'd learned to grab every opportunity with both hands, especially if it meant having the chance to say 'thank you'.

Dad and I sat in the garden and wrote a speech together, and then a couple of weeks later we were stood outside Westminster Abbey, this iconic, gothic church where Prince William and Kate had got married.

The spires soared toward the sky, massive stained-glass windows twinkled in the sunlight. I must have looked nervous because my nurse Jenny said, 'Don't worry, you'll be fine. I'm going to wing it.' She'd been invited to speak too, and I felt a sensation of calm wash over me knowing that she was by my side, in the same way she was during all those nights in hospital I couldn't sleep.

We walked up the steps through the grand entrance into the abbey. We were one of the first ones to be allowed in, and the cavernous hall, with its rows of ornate pillars and arches echoed with our voices as our shoes tip-tapped over the chequered floor and we were shown to our seats. We also met Antony for the first time; he was lovely. As the room started to fill up, everyone was talking in hushed tones, and I remember thinking it was really quiet despite the hundreds of people. I kept an eye on the programme throughout the service. Before me there were introductions to some special people who'd been invited, including having to stand for the Countess of Wessex; hymns sung by the Westminster Abbey Special Service Choir and a speech by Olive Belfield, a daughter of a nurse who worked for the NHS when it was first formed and who followed in her mum's footsteps to become a nurse herself. Before I knew it, it was our turn to take to the podium. I remember walking up the steps with Jenny in front of the gathered two thousand-strong crowd, and feeling so sick.

'Just breathe, just speak,' I told myself.

Jenny gave me an encouraging smile, and I felt so much comfort knowing that she was there with me. I took a deep breath, and looked at the paper in front of me. In that moment, the speech was transformed from words on a page to a deep thank you from the bottom of my heart as I thought about how grateful I was to the NHS – I thought about Beth, Jenny and all the other nurses who had gone above and beyond the call of duty to care for me; the surgeons, doctors and dentists who had pieced me back together; the physios and occupational therapists who had given me the gift of movement again, and everyone from the porters to the children's playworkers, who worked tirelessly to get me back home. But, most importantly, I thought about the hope they had given to my family. I can't begin to imagine how upset they must have been as I lay in a coma, and the support which had been given to them during those darkest hours had brought so much comfort. If my family were happy, then I was happy, and to see them smiling again was all I cared about.

As I said my final words, there was a moment of silence, and then the abbey filled with rapturous applause. I looked at Jenny in shock, as we were told you weren't allowed to clap in Westminster Abbey, but here everyone was on their feet.

Jenny said a few words, and then we hugged as the room echoed with the sound of clapping once again. We walked back to our seats and Mum and Dad looked

at me, crying. We sat for the rest of service in silence, reflecting on the journey we had been on.

Afterwards, all us speakers, including Bart's Hospital Trauma Surgeon Martin Griffiths, who I'd met at the NHS Hero Awards, stood in a line, as Sophie, Countess of Wessex, came to meet us.

She was kind enough to say to me, 'You were so inspiring,' shaking my hand while I smiled back at her, shyly. Afterwards, a swarm of people lined up to speak with me, saying the kindest words, and I realised, 'I have just spoken at Westminster Abbey, I can tell my children when I am older.' It was one of the first times I had allowed myself to look to the future, and I felt so honoured that I had been chosen to speak and share my gratitude for the NHS with the world.

A few days later, we were contacted by RAF officer Harriet Curtis-Lowe, who'd founded the One Voice project. She'd started the initiative following her experiences while serving in Afghanistan and its original aim was to bring together people of every faith – including Hindu, Muslim, Buddhist, Christian – and those of no faith, from the UK armed forces to record a song called 'A Path to Peace'. Following the success of the single, and a documentary, the project started working with schools to spread the message of tolerance and understanding.

Now, she was recording another single and wanted me to be involved. I felt so honoured to be asked, and

knew that in the wake of the bomb, the message was more important than ever. Harry Styles' motto is: 'Treat people with kindness.' Such a simple message, but one which I'd always tried to live my life by. I love RE, learning about different cultures, and always thought it was important to treat people equally. But, before May 22nd, I was never really vocal with my views. For example, if I heard someone saying a homophobic comment, I would be angry about it in my head, but would never have the courage to say anything out loud. But, after the attack, when I witnessed all the hate toward the Muslim community in the press, on social media, in the street, it really hit me that I wanted to make the world a better place. I wanted to stand up and tell everyone that I didn't believe the suicide bomber was a representative for other Muslims for a second, that I would never blame Islam for what had happened, and that we were all equal. I don't hate any religion after what happened – if anything, it has made me love and appreciate everyone in the world even more. The way that everyone came together made me realise how truly amazing people are, no matter what they believe in, and that, ultimately, there is more good in the world than bad.

By taking part in the single, I wanted to show everyone that I wasn't afraid, that the attack hadn't made me frightened or judgmental – it was the opposite.

By the time Christmas came around, I'd been made an ambassador for the High Sheriff of Manchester and, through my role, had spoken passionately at mental health awareness events about the importance of talking and sharing on wellbeing. I couldn't believe it when I – yes, little old me – was asked to present The Student Awards at the annual prizegiving event at the Bridgewater School in Manchester. I was following in the footsteps of the actor Henry Winkler, who, as my parents excitedly told me, had played The Fonz in the hit eighties sitcom *Happy Days*. I looked him up on YouTube and thought he looked very cool in his leather jacket with turned-up collar.

I'd also been very lucky to win both the Amplifon Young Hero and Overall Hero Awards – which celebrate acts of courage, bravery and selflessness, and was presented by Falklands war survivor Simon Weston CBE and police officer Wayne Marques, who fought off terrorists in the London Bridge attack. I felt truly humbled to be in the presence of such bravery.

And, finally, I had made it to Clarence House for afternoon tea with the Duchess of Cornwall.

Snuggling in next to me, she said, 'Oh my gosh, look at you!' The last time she'd seen me, I was in a wheelchair with a big frame on my arm. Now here I was, confidently walking, free of casts and frame and fear. It had been a whirlwind year, and I was so grateful that I'd been given these chances to share my

experiences, to say thank you and to give something back. And, from awards to afternoon tea, Nell was always in my thoughts, reminding me every day that I needed to make the most of every moment, for the both of us.

CHAPTER FORTY

What Makes Us Stronger

The saying goes: what doesn't kill you, makes you stronger.

It's been several years now since the attack, and I've had a lot of time to reflect on what that statement means to me.

Before 22 May 2017, I was not strong. In fact, I was the complete opposite: I was a wuss. I was scared of needles, I hated exercise, I lacked the confidence to stand up for my beliefs. I wanted to conform, follow the crowd, blend in. But everything I've experienced since the attack has, bit by bit, changed my perspective on life. I no longer had the choice to fade into the background. I was one of the hundreds of victims of the Manchester Arena bomb attack – my photo in the paper for all to see as I fought for my life in hospital. I could either give up and allow myself to be consumed by fear and anger, or see it as a second chance in life,

to grab hold of every opportunity that came my way, to understand how lucky I was – how lucky we as a family were – that I survived when others didn't.

I chose the latter.

I've been asked time and again: 'Where does this inner strength come from?' Was it not being killed, like the saying goes? No. I don't think it came from surviving, or from anywhere inside me – I think it came from *around* me. When I was little, Mum told me that my name meant the Goddess of Love. As cheesy as this may sound, it's love that made me strong.

The moment the attack happened, I was engulfed in love – from the strangers who helped save my life and subsequently became my close friends; from the people of Manchester who all pulled together when the city was at its lowest ebb; from the royals, politicians and stars of screen and stage who took time to show that they cared; from my community in Holmes Chapel who rallied around us; from the hundreds of donations and messages from around the world; from my friends who showered me in support; from the kind gestures from Nell's parents even though they were nursing their own heartbreak; and from my devoted family who never left my side. *People* make us stronger: community, kindness, love.

My memories of Nell are so closely linked to these sentiments. I'll never forget our final moments, as she linked her arm in mine, her face full of so much joy,

as she said, 'I love you.' She was the happiest I'd ever seen her, and I'm honoured that I was able to share that moment with her. There isn't a day that goes by when I don't miss her immensely and don't think about how different life would be if she was still by my side supporting me. I will, however, take her ridiculous sense of humour and resilience with me everywhere I go in life, and I'll keep continuing to learn to accept what has happened to me, and to not let it define me, but instead shape the way I live.

I value life a lot more now: the small things. I'll get happy over a cup of tea or a pair of shoes. I still remember that moment in the Burns Unit when I saw the brilliant blue of the sky for the first time, looking at it as if it were the eighth wonder of the world. I'm not taking things for granted any more. Before the attack, I'd grown out of telling my parents how much I loved them. Now I hug them at least five times a day! I hold my friends close; a legacy to Nell.

But, though I've become confident and content in so many ways, I'd be lying if I didn't admit that the one area I still struggle with is my scars.

Unfortunately, there was not a place on my body that wasn't affected by the attack. In this day and age, social media is the main focus in a teenager's life and, even though I hold so many other things to be more important now, it's something I can't escape

from. Before the attack, I felt incredibly self-conscious about being in my own skin and I do believe that that was partially down to the fact that I felt pressured to look, act and dress a certain way. So, already being an incredibly self-conscious teenager, I didn't know how to cope with all the scars that I had accumulated all over my body. When I looked at myself in the mirror, I almost couldn't recognise myself as my mind was overwhelmed with insecurities. In all honesty, these feelings of embarrassment and shame are things that still occur on a day-to-day basis and I still feel the need to cover up all of my scars as much as possible. Luckily, I have the most amazing and supportive family and friends who encourage me to embrace my appearance and to care less about what others think. I have a whiteboard in my room, and Mum writes me little notes of positivity every day:

'You are amazing'

'You inspire me every day.'

'You are a fighter.'

That's what Mum calls me, her little fighter. I was born seven weeks prematurely, and Mum always says that I came into the world fighting and haven't stopped.

'I feel so proud of you,' she tells me. 'If you hadn't coped with things the way you had, then we wouldn't be here now.'

It's her strength and belief in me that makes me feel sure that one day I will feel confident with the way I look.

*

I still have days where I feel like I'm under a raincloud – some days, the grief hits me so hard I feel like I will topple over. And that's OK – it's OK to be sad, and to talk about it when we feel that way. But, when it's time to pick myself up, I think of Nell saying 'Get on with it, Freya Lewis!' and I dry my tears and put on a smile.

There were moments on 22 May 2017 when I thought I was going to die. In those moments, I thought of all the things that filled me with happiness and love. To have any sort of future feels like such a luxury, but I know I have to strive for it to be filled with more of those things: they are what's important in life. I dream that I'll be an actress and a mother with a nice fluffy dog and my precious family close by, I dream of a life filled with music, doing the things that make me happy.

I wish it hadn't taken the attack to make this all so clear to me. What we lost that night, we can never get back. It took one man to rip so many lives in two, but it also created ripples of a community that stretched all over our planet, and for a time it felt like Manchester was the epicentre of one wonderful, connected world. We don't have to experience terrorist attacks to learn how to live in this way, and if I could ask you to take anything away from this book it is that you choose

to embrace the power of community and connection, which bring with them so much strength, and which have given me so much to live for.

That list of people who helped me after the attack and who made me stronger now includes you, reader, for letting me tell you my story. I'm so grateful.

A Poem for Nell Jones

I miss you so much, more than you'll ever know.
I miss you talking about boys – for example, Joe.
I miss the way you fell on us when you laugh.
I miss being jealous of how smart you were at maths.
I miss you always going on about Ariana and Ed.
I miss you speaking to me on FaceTime for hours, sat
 on your bed.
I miss you squeezing my hand whenever you got
 excited.
I miss your glasses and complaints about being
 short-sighted.
I miss you singing along with me to people like Harry.
I miss you being the only one to admit it's he I'd marry.
I miss our calls on all your brand-new phones.
I will, and always will love you, my gorgeous Nell Jones.

by Freya Lewis, 17 July 2017

ACKNOWLEDGEMENTS

This book wouldn't have been possible without my dear friend, Amisha Desai, who has been my incredible ghostwriter. Because of you, every thought, idea and dream of mine has been displayed beautifully within each page of this story. You've captured everything in the exact way I imagined, but most importantly, you've become part of the Lewis family, and such an important friend to me; for that, I cannot thank you enough. You are the very core of this book, and I love you beyond words.

Thanks to everyone at Orion. It was my dream to be able write a book about my experiences, and you were willing to listen to my story and believed it was something other people would want to read.

Kim and Phil Dick – I owe everything to you. Without the two of you, my story would have ended right there in the Arena. You were the people who came to my

rescue and took care of me when others just walked past I feel privileged to have met two people who have the biggest hearts and souls. Quite simply, you saved my life and I wouldn't be here without you.

Everyone from the emergency services who helped saved my life on that fateful night – the strength and serenity that you all displayed was exceptional. I would never have imagined such professionalism and kindness on a night full of horror and uncertainty; you're all superheroes. Especially WPC Clare Smith, who held my hand the whole time, and still continues to support our family – thank you so much.

Everyone at Royal Manchester Children's Hospital and University Dental Hospital of Manchester – there are too many of you to acknowledge individually, but you know who you are. Thank you for making my hospital journey full of hope, care and, at some points, laughter. I constantly thank my lucky stars that I was taken to the most loving hospital in the world, which still continues to look after me amazingly. You are the reason why my family and I call the hospital our second home.

To all of the amazing people who supported the One Love Manchester fund. Through your kindness and generosity you have changed the lives of so many, including myself. You have helped shape my future; thank you, from the bottom of my heart.

There are no words to express how grateful my family

and I are to Royal Manchester Childrens Hospital and Ronald MacDonald House and we continue to support their respective charities in any way we can.

Special thanks to my medical team:

- Matt Nixon, my lead surgeon. You've kept the Lewis family together and laughing during the most difficult of times. You have shown us the very best that humanity has to offer, it has been an absolute honour to know you.
- Jenny Grant, my HDU nurse. You're the funniest Northern girl I know. You sat with me when I was at my lowest. You did more than just your job, you became a friend.
- Beth Booth, my ICU nurse. You looked after my family when I couldn't. You've been so kind and caring and also have been adopted by us!
- Angela Schofield and Jo May, my amazing dental team at RMCH. You've both been through every second of my journey and helped me return to my old self. You're both so incredible!
- Martin Ashley, Tamsin Cooper and Julian Yates, my dental team at University Dental Hospital of Manchester: you helped complete my journey and held my hand throughout every step! (Tamsin – literally!)

Saying 'thank you' isn't enough for all of you! I hope you know how grateful my family and I are.

Jenny and Lee, my acting teachers – thank you for impacting my life so greatly, and continuing to support me as my adoptive aunt and uncle!

Barbara Morris-Brown – you're my absolute rock. I couldn't have gotten through any of my life post-hospital without you. You'll always be in my life, for ever and more.

Carol Chaddock and Jack Curr – thank you to Carol for putting me back on my feet and thank you to Jack for helping me grow stronger! (Even though I still hate exercise.)

The community of Holmes Chapel and all of my friends – thank you for making such a lovely place for me to return to. You've all supported our family in more ways than we could've imagined; I'm beyond privileged to call this village my home.

We have experienced unprecedented kindness and generosity from people from all over the world, and we especially recognise the warmth and continued support we have received from HRH The Duchess of Cornwall.

And, finally, a few words for my best friends, other-wise known as the Lewis family. People always ask me 'How did you get through everything?' I always reply with the same answer: because of my wonderful family. I couldn't have asked for a better bunch of people to be by my side every step of the way. You all have mentally and physically held me together throughout every up and down. You all have kept me laughing

at anything and everything, no matter how dark the humour may be. You all were the reason I opened up about everything, I walked again, I smiled again and why I chose to fight for my life. I wouldn't be where I am without you. I love you more than anything else in the world.

When people ask what made me stronger, it was this list of people.